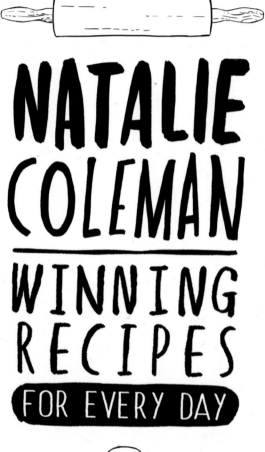

NATALIE COLEMAN

WINNING RECIPES

FOR EVERY DAY

NATALIE

WINNING

COLEMAN

RECIPES

FOR EVERY DAY

Quercus

CONTENTS

INTRODUCTION

GOOD HOME-COOKED FOOD HAS BEEN PART OF MY LIFE FOR AS FAR BACK AS I CAN REMEMBER.

At school, I was one of the lucky kids who had a mum that made me a packed lunch every day. I was never subjected to the horror of lumpy mashed potatoes that were spooned on to the dinner plate using an ice-cream scoop; or spam; or custard that was so thick I'm surprised it didn't clog up your digestive system; or any of the other weapons of school dinner destruction that were inflicted on my schoolmates. Mum used to mix it up a bit, but I remember loving the mini pitta breads filled with Cheddar and cucumber slices. The cheese had to be a certain thickness otherwise it was too cheesy and got a bit claggy on the back of your throat, and the cucumber not so thick that the pitta bread became a doughy soggy mess in your hands. It sounds weird, especially for a 7-year-old kid, but I've always appreciated the art of precision.

I was quite a lively kid too. I had a habit of climbing on kitchen surfaces then falling from them and cracking my head open. This happened on a few occasions. One of the times I did this, I was in search of ice-cream cones. Instead of asking one of my parents to help me, I wanted to get them myself. I've always been an assertive kind of girl.

Growing up, most weekends were spent with my nan and grandad. Saturdays were always the same: shopping on the Roman Road with my nan, mum, sister and sometimes my auntie Linda. We looked at the same old tat week in week out, but it was a ritual. We would pit stop in the indoor café and my nan would have tea and toast and me and my sister would be allowed chips as a treat – mine drowned in ketchup and hers plain. I've never really known anybody not like ketchup, but my sister hates it; even the smell of it makes her ill. We would also visit the 'chocolate man' as I called him. He was the Willy Wonka of the Roman Road. He stocked all kinds of sweets and chocolates, but I always went for the same thing – a chocolate bar with a strawberry filling. One weekend we went to the Roman Road and the chocolate man wasn't there. He wasn't there the following week either and by week three I was in mourning. He never came back and I've never seen that strawberry chocolate bar on sale anywhere else.

My nan was the most amazing cook and could make anything taste good. If we were at Nan's on Sundays, like clockwork she and my mum would serve up our roast dinner with all the trimmings. I couldn't eat my roast without mint jelly. It didn't matter what meat we had, I had to have mint jelly on my roasties, and if it wasn't there I went without. Nan's corned beef pie was legendary. We would all lurk in the hallway to get the first slice and as soon as the dish hit the table it was gone. She also baked lots of cakes and other goodies, and if me and my sister were around, we would always want to get involved, which inevitably would end up with us turning our Sunday best outfits into something from a kitchen warzone. Looking back, most of my childhood memories revolve around food and the family being together and I'm sure this is where my love of cooking comes from.

My aunt Ellen was the one who suggested I apply for *MasterChef*, and she must have had an in-built annual reminder in her diary because I filled in the questionnaire for three years in a row. The first two years I heard nothing, then the third year a researcher from Shine TV called about my application. I stuttered my way through a 20-minute interview but didn't hear back. Year four, application completed, again I had a phone call, but this time the researcher was asking if I could come for a screen test and audition. I had to take along a cold dish to plate up in front of the researchers and casting team. I made a vanilla panna cotta with honey-roasted peaches, raspberry coulis and almond crumble. I didn't even really know what a panna cotta was, but it sounded impressive and I thought that my take on peach melba was pretty special. At the end of the audition

I was told I might get a call, or I wouldn't hear from anything as they couldn't give feedback to the thousands of applicants. I heard nothing.

Another year went by. After my nan died, I used to go round and cook for my grandad, so he became the taster for all my 'training'. Grandad's dinners went from basic fish and chips or pie and mash to boeuf bourguignon and luxury fish pies. I had started a form of cooking boot camp training and Grandad was becoming a lean, mean, eating machine. My hands were covered in burns and cuts but my grandad was happy. Year five came and I managed to get through the same stages as the previous year. But this time, the call I was anxiously waiting for did come. I ran out into the office stairwell to be told that I was one of the lucky 50 who would make up that year's contestants on the 'journey that will change your life'.

MY NAN BELLA

It was a freezing cold, rainy October morning when I crossed the river and made my way to the *MasterChef* studios for the first time. I was led into the contestant holding room, which was to become my second home. I spent so much time there in between rounds trying to do my thinking face for the camera as well as hold it together and not turn into a jibbering, blubbing mess.

Being propelled into the scary, stressful, exciting world of food and the *MasterChef* competition for six weeks seemed like a dream. I was constantly pinching myself to see if I would wake up. From my first invention test and my slop of a stir-fry, to cooking for Marcus Wareing, Michael Caines and the chefs'

table, then making the poshest doner kebab in a three-star Michelin restaurant in Florence; it all felt so unreal. And never in a million years did I think I'd win, but of course it was a perfect end to the perfect dream. And in a cheesy fashion I've now had IX tattooed on my wrist. I think of it as my lucky number. I won series nine; the heat I was in was nine of ten; my locker at the studio, which I chose without thinking, was nine; the day before the final I turned off the timer for my hazelnut crumble biscuits on 0.09 seconds; and to top that off the house I grew up in was number nine. It just seems that nine is a magic number for me.

NAN'S FAMOUS
CORNED BEEF HASH PIE

After filming finished, life had to go back to normal until the series was broadcast. I hate secrets and lies and can't really keep much quiet for long, but I had to hold in the biggest secret of my life. I went back to work, but what I thought would be a two- to three-month wait until I could sing from the rooftops turned out to be over five months because the series airing date kept changing. But somehow I managed, and when the final aired on the 2nd May 2013 my tears erupted like a volcano in overdrive. Suddenly everything was real.

By then I was simply thinking about what was next. All I wanted was a job in a kitchen; I wanted to take advantage of this amazing opportunity. And I have gone on to do things most people would tear their right arm off to do. We were told on the evening of the final day of filming that we would be helping to write the *MasterChef* cookbook, and if you'd ever told me that I would one day have a book in the shops I would have laughed you out of town.

The *MasterChef* team help finalists find their way into the food world, so I presented the amazing Karen Ross with a list of about 30 Michelin-starred chefs I wanted to do a 'stage' with ('stage' is a posh French word for unpaid work experience). It was like a very ambitious kid's Christmas list and even Karen thought I was being optimistic, but if you don't ask. So a few days later, Santa Claus (Karen) had worked magic and the following week I was in Michel Roux Jr's kitchen at Le Gavroche, podding peas and turning potatoes. I then went on to meet many of my heroes and work in

their kitchens for anything from three days to a whole week. I podded a lot of peas but sometimes I got to be on the pass, plating up two-star Michelin food. I am very lucky to say that I have worked with the likes of Tom Kitchin, Tom Kerridge, Daniel Clifford, Nuno Mendes, Simon Rogan and Marcus Wareing, and I still can't really believe it's happened to a girl like me.

My aim with this book is for you to be able to sit back and think 'hey, I can do that too. That recipe may sound unknown, hard, posh or scary, but I am going to give it a shot'. I'm above all a home cook and I still have a long way to go before I can call myself a chef. I've never had any training – I've learned through marathon sessions of watching cookery shows, reading books and watching videos online, and I've had as many disasters as triumphs along the way.

But if I can do it you can too. Throughout the book I want to share with you what I have learned and give you the recipes that I hope will inspire you to cook every day. Because above all food is fun and something to be shared with your friends and family. It should not be a chore or something you fear, nor should it be about perfect *MasterChef*-style dishes. You'll make mistakes, as I have, but by making those mistakes you become a better cook. So have fun, be adventurous, remember that rustic is good, and get the kids stuck in... Nothing beats the satisfaction of eating something you've cooked yourself or sharing that pleasure with others.

I CONSIDER THIS CHAPTER MY SPECIAL TREATS SECTION,

so what better way to start my book than with some of my absolute favourite things to eat?! Yes, if we were to eat fried food every day we'd all end up the size of a house, but as the old saying goes: 'everything in moderation'. When done right, frying gives beautiful crispness, not greasy wetness, as the hot oil draws out all the extra moisture during the cooking process.

You can pick up a deep-fat fryer really cheaply these days and I do think it's worth investing in one, though you can still achieve the same results using a deep, solid saucepan and an oil thermometer. You just need to pay close attention to regulate the temperature as this method is not as consistent as using a fryer. And whether you're using a machine or a pan, be VERY CAREFUL as hot oil is HOT! Don't leave it unattended at any point, turn on your extractor fan, and keep kids and pets out of the kitchen. Once you've finished, let the oil cool down before you try to move the pan and never pour it down the sink or you'll end up with a big fat plumber's bill for your blocked drains – put it into some kind of used packaging or container and throw that away.

I've included all the fried treats I really love here, including my twist on Spanish croquettes (I've given mine a British flavour), juicy lamb koftas inspired by late-night snacks after a big night out, and irresistible dippy doughnuts, which I could quite happily dunk every day in gooey chocolate or caramel sauce. And of course I couldn't leave out one of my favourite things in life, Scotch eggs, which I served as part of my winning *MasterChef* menu. You just can't beat a good Scotch egg and there are so many different variations you can try when it comes to fillings and flavours. I've included my top three versions here; I hope you enjoy them as much as I do!

MY CHAMPION SCOTCH EGGS

MAKES 4

6 medium eggs
450g good-quality sausage
    meat
1 tbsp wholegrain mustard
2 tbsp finely chopped
    parsley
Leaves from 2 thyme sprigs
50g plain flour
100g regular or panko
    breadcrumbs
Vegetable oil, for frying
Ice cubes
Salt and pepper
Piccalilli Sauce (see page 213),
    to serve

EQUIPMENT
Deep-fat fryer (or a deep
    saucepan and an oil
    thermometer)

My winning menu on *MasterChef* included a black pudding Scotch egg. After that, all my friends wanted to taste my Scotch eggs. I love cooking (and eating!) these so much and I'm always up for trying different ingredients and flavours. Here's a classic one, and I hope you enjoy my variations on the next page.

 Fill a saucepan two-thirds full with water (or deep enough to cover the eggs), bring to the boil, then put in four of the eggs (still in their shells) and boil for 5 minutes for a very runny yolk, 6 minutes for a runny yolk or 8 minutes for a hard yolk.

 While the eggs are cooking, fill a medium mixing bowl with cold water and add two handfuls of ice cubes.

❸ When the eggs are cooked as you want them, remove from the saucepan using a slotted spoon and place straight into the iced water to cool for 5 minutes. This stops the eggs cooking further.

 In a food processor, blitz the sausage meat, mustard, parsley and thyme until well combined. Season with just a little salt – not too generously as the sausage meat may already have some seasoning – and a good crack of black pepper. Divide into four even-sized balls and chill in the fridge for 15 minutes to firm up.

❺ Cut eight squares of cling film, 20cm x 20cm. You need two per sausage ball. When the meat mixture has firmed up, place a sausage ball on top of one square of cling film and place another square on top. Using the palm of your hand, flatten the ball to the thickness of a pound coin. Repeat with the rest of the sausage balls.

❻ Whisk the two remaining eggs in a bowl. Place the flour in another bowl and the breadcrumbs in a third bowl.

 Peel the boiled eggs. If they're tricky to peel, try doing it under a cold running tap, which helps remove the shell without damaging the egg. When peeled, dab them on a piece of kitchen roll to remove any excess water and pieces of shell. Roll the eggs in the flour.

8 Remove the top square of cling film from one piece of sausage meat and place an egg in the middle of the meat mixture. Gather together all the corners of the bottom square of cling film and use it to carefully ease the meat around the egg so it is completely covered. Remove the cling film.

9 Now roll the ball first in the flour, then in the egg and finally in the breadcrumbs. It should have a good coating of breadcrumbs, so if it looks a little thin after your first attempt, re-dip it in the egg and then the breadcrumbs.

10 Repeat steps 8 and 9 with the remaining eggs and sausage meat.

11 Preheat a deep-fat fryer to 170°C (or use a deep, heavy-based saucepan and an oil thermometer to regulate the temperature). Fry two eggs at a time for 7 minutes, turning occasionally so that they cook evenly and the breadcrumbs don't burn.

12 Once cooked, remove using a slotted spoon and drain on kitchen paper to remove excess oil. The Scotch eggs can be served hot or at room temperature.

MORE FLAVOURS THIS WAY

MORE FLAVOURS

CHORIZO SCOTCH EGGS

To make **Chorizo Scotch Eggs**, follow the recipe on the previous pages, using 250g sausage meat (rather than 450g) and adding 200g cooking chorizo (skin removed). Omit the mustard and thyme, but keep the parsley and all the other ingredients as before. Follow the method as described, adding the chorizo in with the sausage meat to the food processor. Serve with mayo mixed with paprika.

SMOKED MACKEREL SCOTCH EGGS

To make **Smoked Mackerel Scotch Eggs**, omit the sausage meat, mustard, parsley and thyme, and instead use 175g smoked mackerel, 175g mashed potato (no butter or cream), 2 tablespoons of roughly chopped chives, 2 tablespoons of roughly chopped parsley, 2 roughly chopped spring onions and 1 teaspoon of horseradish sauce. Remove the skin from the mackerel, de-bone and flake it, then add it to the food processor with all these ingredients and blitz to combine well. Follow the method for cooking and coating the eggs and frying, as described on the previous page. Serve these with mayo or crème fraîche mixed with horseradish.

FRIED GREEN tomatoes WITH SALSA

SERVES 4–6

FOR THE TOMATOES

4 large green tomatoes (or
  beef tomatoes), cut into
  1cm slices
150g self-raising flour
Pinch of cayenne pepper
75g fine cornmeal
2 eggs, beaten
150ml whole milk
Vegetable oil, for frying
Salt and pepper

FOR THE SALSA

4 plum tomatoes, peeled
  (see Tip), deseeded and
  cut into 1cm dice
1 avocado, skin and stone
  removed, cut into 1cm
  dice
3 tbsp finely chopped
  coriander
½ red onion, finely
  chopped
1 red chilli, finely chopped
  (deseeded if less heat is
  desired)
Grated zest and juice of
  1 lime
Salt and pepper

I know it's cheesy but I love the film *Fried Green Tomatoes at the Whistle Stop Café*. The tomatoes they serve look so delicious that I've always wanted to dive into the TV and grab them. When I found green tomatoes on sale at Borough Market, I thought I'd try my hand at recreating those amazing-looking fried goodies made famous by the film. You can find green tomatoes in most greengrocers; look for heritage or heirloom tomatoes.

1 Put the green tomato slices into a colander and place the colander in a bowl. Sprinkle the tomatoes with salt, to draw out the excess water, and leave for 45 minutes.

2 Meanwhile, mix all the salsa ingredients in a small bowl and season with salt and pepper. Allow to stand for 30 minutes at room temperature so the tomatoes take on the flavours.

3 When the green tomato slices have had their 45 minutes in the colander, rinse with cold water and pat dry using kitchen paper.

4 In a large mixing bowl, combine the self-raising flour, cayenne pepper and cornmeal, and season with salt and pepper. Whisk in the beaten eggs and milk, until you have a smooth batter. Leave to stand for 15 minutes.

5 Heat a large, deep frying pan with vegetable oil (2cm deep) over a medium–high heat. In batches, dip the tomatoes in the batter to coat, then fry in the vegetable oil for 2 minutes on each side, until golden and crispy. Remove from the pan using a slotted spoon and drain on kitchen paper.

6 Keep the cooked tomatoes warm under foil or in a low oven while you fry the rest. Serve with the salsa.

TIP When peeling tomatoes, make a small cross across the stalk of each tomato. Put in a bowl and cover with boiling water. Leave for 1–2 minutes until the skin is starting to peel back. Plunge into cold water, peel away the skin and discard.

VEGETABLE CRISPS

SERVES 4

2 large parsnips, peeled
2 raw beetroots, peeled
2 carrots, peeled
2 Jerusalem artichokes,
    peeled
Vegetable oil, for frying
Fine salt

EQUIPMENT
Deep-fat fryer (or a
    deep saucepan and
    oil thermometer)

This is a perfect way to use up any vegetables lying around in your cupboard that may otherwise go to waste. Make sure to drain the crisps on kitchen paper and keep the batches separate so that the cooked crisps don't soak up excess grease from the next batch. These are best eaten fresh.

1. Preheat a deep-fat fryer to 180°C (or use a deep, heavy-based saucepan and an oil thermometer to regulate the temperature).

2. Using a vegetable peeler, peel off thin slices from the vegetables to make shavings. Let the shavings rest for 30 minutes on kitchen paper to allow any moisture to escape.

3. Separate into batches of the different vegetables and fry for 1–2 minutes until golden and crisp, leaving the beetroot until last in case its colour runs into the oil. The beetroot can take 2–4 minutes to cook.

4. Drain the crisps on kitchen paper and season with fine salt. Do not pile the freshly cooked batches on top of already cooked crisps, or they will absorb the excess grease and become soggy. Serve immediately.

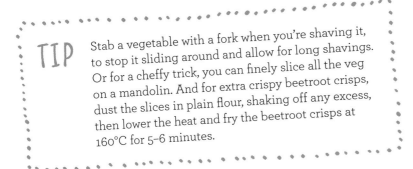

TIP Stab a vegetable with a fork when you're shaving it, to stop it sliding around and allow for long shavings. Or for a cheffy trick, you can finely slice all the veg on a mandolin. And for extra crispy beetroot crisps, dust the slices in plain flour, shaking off any excess, then lower the heat and fry the beetroot crisps at 160°C for 5–6 minutes.

GREEN PEPPERCORN SQUID with GINGER DIPPING SAUCE

When I was a DJ, I used to run a club night called MOOCH with my best mate Ed. Before a gig, we would take our guest DJs out for dinner on the Kingsland Road in Shoreditch, where we were spoilt for choice with all the amazing Vietnamese restaurants. We always ordered crispy squid to start, so this recipe brings back great memories! It's best to buy cleaned squid to save time (ask the fishmonger) and stick to baby or small ones, as larger squid can be chewy and take a lot longer to cook.

SERVES 4 AS A STARTER

FOR THE SQUID
600g baby or small squid including tentacles (roughly 8–10cm long), cleaned
75g cornflour
75g plain flour
1 tbsp Maldon sea salt
2 tbsp green peppercorns
Vegetable oil, for frying
3 spring onions, finely sliced, to serve (optional)
Lemon or lime wedges, to serve

FOR THE DIPPING SAUCE
1 tbsp groundnut or vegetable oil
3 tbsp light soy sauce
4 tbsp rice wine vinegar
1 tbsp palm sugar or caster sugar
Juice of ½ lime
4cm piece of ginger, peeled and grated
1 garlic clove, crushed
1 red chilli, finely sliced (optional for extra heat)

EQUIPMENT
Deep-fat fryer (or a deep saucepan and oil thermometer)

1 First, make the dipping sauce, at least 30 minutes before serving to allow the flavours time to develop. In a small bowl, mix together all the ingredients until well combined, and set aside. For extra heat you can add the finely sliced red chilli.

2 Then begin preparing the squid. You can get cleaned squid from supermarkets or, if buying from a fishmonger, ask them to do it for you. However, still check the squid before you cook, as sometimes there is a little sand inside the tubes. Cut open the squid tube by slicing up one side – you will see a natural line/marking to use as a guide – and open it out flat. Using the back of your knife, scrape off any sand or dirt that may be left inside. If the cartilage is still there, remove it and discard. Rinse under cold water then pat dry on kitchen paper.

3 Turn the squid over and, using a serrated knife, criss-cross the surface, being careful not to cut all the way through the flesh. Set aside for a moment.

4 In a large bowl, mix the cornflour, plain flour and salt. Using a pestle and mortar, crush the green peppercorns so they are about a third of their original size, then add to the bowl of flour and mix in.

5 Preheat a deep-fat fryer to 180°C (or use a deep, heavy-based saucepan and an oil thermometer to regulate the temperature).

6 When prepped, dip the squid into the flour, shake off the excess and place them in a tray.

CONTINUES

CONTINUED

7 When the oil is ready, use tongs to add the squid in batches of two tubes and two tentacles at a time. (You don't want to cook too much at once or it will stick together and the oil temperature will drop, resulting in inedible soggy, oily squid instead of the nice crispy finish you're after.) Cook each batch for 2–3 minutes until the squid becomes crispy, then remove with the tongs and drain on kitchen paper.

8 Cook the rest of the squid in batches. Try not to put the freshly cooked batch on top of the previous batch as it will absorb any excess oil. You can keep it warm in a low oven.

9 When you have finished cooking, place all the squid on a serving platter and season with a pinch of salt. Scatter over the finely chopped spring onions, if using, and serve with the dipping sauce and lemon or lime wedges.

COURGETTE FRITTERS *WITH* MINT CRÈME *FRAÎCHE*

MAKES 15

FOR THE FRITTERS
600g courgettes (3–4)
1 small red onion, peeled
1 tbsp finely chopped
    parsley
1 tsp baking powder
3 eggs, beaten
1 tbsp milk
100g plain flour
50g feta cheese, crumbled
Vegetable oil, for frying
Salt and pepper

FOR THE MINT
CRÈME FRAÎCHE
300ml crème fraîche
Leaves from 4 mint sprigs,
    finely sliced
Squeeze of lemon juice

Fritters make a brilliant starter or vegetarian main course. They are also a clever way of getting kids to eat their veggies as the healthy stuff is hidden in the batter mix. Don't miss the variation I've given opposite for sweetcorn fritters – if you're feeling fritter-happy you can make some of both. Fritters are definitely best dipped, so I really recommend making the accompaniments I've included here. And remember to wring out the excess liquid from the mixture or you'll end up with a pan of soggy veg.

1 Cut off the tops and bottoms of the courgettes. Place a clean tea towel or muslin cloth on a work surface, and grate the courgettes onto it.

2 Chop the onion in half and grate it into the tea towel or muslin. Bring together the corners of the cloth and wring it over the sink to strain out all the excess water from the vegetables. Once strained, empty the veg into a mixing bowl.

3 Add the parsley and baking powder, and season with salt and pepper. Add the beaten eggs and the milk. Sift in the flour and mix it all together well. The mixture will be very dense and thick. Finally, add the crumbled feta and mix well.

4 Heat a large frying pan on a medium–high heat with vegetable oil (1cm deep).

5 Spoon the courgette batter into the oil in circles about 8cm across and 5mm thick. You should be able to fit in two or three at a time. Make sure the mixture is not too thick, or it may not cook all the way through.

6 After 2–3 minutes on the first side, when the mixture starts to set and brown underneath, flip the fritters over and cook for a further 2–3 minutes. When cooked, remove with a slotted spoon and drain on kitchen paper.

7 Mix the crème fraîche with the sliced mint and a squeeze of lemon, season with a little salt and serve on the side for dipping.

VARIATION

To make Sweetcorn Fritters with Coriander & Chilli
Soured Cream, follow the recipe opposite, omitting the feta
cheese and substituting the courgette, onion and parsley with
a 340g tin of sweetcorn and 4 finely sliced spring onions. Mix
together the fritter ingredients and cook as described. Serve
with soured cream, sprinkled with finely chopped coriander
(leaves of 2 sprigs) and finely sliced red chilli (deseeded).

HAM & CHEDDAR CROQUETTES with MUSTARD MAYO

MAKES 20

FOR THE CROQUETTES

70g butter
Splash of olive oil
1 medium onion, finely
    diced
150g cooked ham hock,
    cut into 1cm dice
70g plain flour, plus extra
    for dusting
500ml whole milk
2 tsp mustard powder
50g Cheddar cheese,
    grated
Vegetable oil, for frying
100g panko breadcrumbs
    (must be panko)
2 large eggs
Salt and pepper

FOR THE MUSTARD MAYO

100g mayonnaise
1 tbsp English mustard

TO SERVE

75g watercress
Juice of 1 lemon
2 tbsp olive oil

EQUIPMENT

Deep-fat fryer (or a
    deep saucepan and
    oil thermometer)

These are inspired by the croquettes I cooked while working at the restaurant Tapas Revolution. Spanish croquettes typically contain Ibérico or Serrano ham, but I wanted to give mine an English twist so I've used ham hock and Cheddar. Panko breadcrumbs are best for the coating because of their fine texture – you can buy them in the world foods section of the supermarket. The mustard mayo gives some extra spice, so dip if you dare!

1 In a large saucepan on a medium heat, melt the butter and a splash of olive oil, then gently soften the onion for 3 minutes. When softened, add the ham hock and cook for a further 2–3 minutes until warmed through.

2 Add the flour and cook for 5 minutes on a low heat to cook it, stirring all the time to prevent the mixture sticking.

3 In a small saucepan on a medium–high heat, warm the milk until nearly at boiling point, then pour into the pan with the ham mixture and gently whisk in.

4 Add the mustard powder, season with salt and pepper, and cook on a gentle heat for 7–8 minutes, until thickened. Remove from the heat and whisk in the cheese.

5 Line a baking tray with cling film, pour in the mixture and cover with cling film. Leave to cool to room temperature, then chill in the fridge for 1 hour to set. When set, remove from the fridge and divide into 20 portions.

6 Preheat a deep-fat fryer to 180°C (or use a deep, heavy-based saucepan and an oil thermometer to regulate the temperature).

7 Place the panko breadcrumbs in a bowl. In another bowl place the eggs and whisk well.

8 Flour your hands and roll each portion of the ham and cheese mix into a ball. Dip first in the egg, then in the breadcrumbs to coat evenly. (A good tip is to keep one hand dry and one hand wet when doing the breadcrumbing, to stop your fingers getting completely covered in sticky breadcrumbs.) Fry the balls in batches of four for 1–2 minutes, until golden. Remove and drain on kitchen paper.

9 When you are ready to serve, mix the mustard with the mayonnaise and place in a small pot or jar for serving. Dress the watercress with the lemon juice and olive oil. Serve the ham croquettes warm with some watercress on the side.

AUBERGINE BHAJIS with TOMATO CHUTNEY

MAKES 12

FOR THE BHAJIS
1 aubergine (about 300g)
½ tsp cumin seeds
200g gram flour
50g self-raising flour
½ tsp turmeric
250ml sparkling water
1 onion, finely sliced
1 red chilli, deseeded and
   finely sliced
2 tbsp finely chopped fresh
   coriander
Vegetable oil, for frying
Salt and pepper

FOR THE CHUTNEY
2 small onions, diced
2 garlic cloves, peeled
   and grated
2 tbsp vegetable oil
4cm piece of ginger, peeled
   and grated
2 tbsp panch phoran (see
   recipe introduction)
2 green chillies, deseeded
   and finely sliced
1 tsp chilli flakes
8 large plum tomatoes,
   deseeded and chopped
50g raisins
2 tbsp sugar
Squeeze of lemon juice

EQUIPMENT
Deep-fat fryer (or a
deep saucepan and oil
thermometer)

This recipe is inspired by Aunty Saira, who I formed a great friendship with on *MasterChef*, and I was lucky enough to try her wonderful street food. Saira's nickname is 'the small aubergine', so instead of the usual onion bhajis I've made mine with aubergines in her honour. When I told her I wanted to include this recipe in my book, she gave me a spice mix called *panch phoran* for flavouring the chutney. You can find it in good Asian stores or mix your own really easily and keep it in a jar. It is made up of equal quantities of five whole spices – cumin seeds, black onion seeds (also known as nigella seeds), black mustard seeds, fennel seeds and fenugreek seeds.

1 First, make the chutney. In a frying pan on a medium heat, cook the onions and garlic with the vegetable oil for about 5 minutes until they begin to brown.

2 Add the ginger, panch phoran, chilli and chilli flakes and cook for a further 3 minutes. Add a splash of water if the chutney begins to look dry.

3 Add the tomatoes, raisins, sugar and squeeze of lemon juice and cook on a gentle heat for 10 minutes until the ingredients begin to break down. Remove from the heat, season with salt and pepper and set aside to let the flavours develop.

4 To prepare the bhajis, remove the stalk from the aubergine and discard it, cut the aubergine into eight wedges and place in a colander in the sink or in a bowl. Sprinkle with 1 tablespoon of salt, place a bowl or plate directly on top of the wedges to weigh them down and leave for 30 minutes.

5 Meanwhile, in a dry frying pan toast the cumin seeds for 1-2 minutes until you can smell them, being careful not to let them burn. Using a pestle and mortar, grind to a powder.

6 After 30 minutes, rinse and pat dry the aubergine, then finely slice it into matchstick strips, 6cm x 0.5cm.

7 Preheat the deep-fat fryer to 180°C (or use a deep, heavy-based saucepan and an oil thermometer to regulate the temperature).

8 In a mixing bowl, combine the gram flour, self-raising flour, turmeric and toasted cumin seeds, then slowly pour in the sparkling water, whisking so it becomes a smooth batter. Add all the remaining ingredients and season with salt and pepper. Mix well so everything is coated.

9 Add tablespoonfuls of the mixture to the fryer, cooking two or three at a time, for 2–3 minutes until golden brown. Use a slotted spoon to remove and drain on kitchen paper.

10 Keep the cooked bhajis warm in a low oven while you fry the rest. Serve warm with the chutney.

LAMB KOFTAS WITH spiced YOGHURT

SERVES 6

FOR THE KOFTAS
1 large red onion,
    finely diced
1kg lamb mince
3 garlic cloves, crushed
1 tbsp dried mint
1 tsp ground cumin
1 large cucumber
Juice of ½ lemon
Olive oil, for frying
Salt and pepper

FOR THE SPICED YOGHURT
250ml natural Greek yoghurt
¼ tsp ground cumin
¼ tsp ground coriander
2 tbsp finely chopped
    coriander
Juice of ½ lemon

TO SERVE
50g pine nuts
8 pitta breads
100g feta, crumbled

After a heavy night out with friends, I've made many a trip to George's kebab shop on Hackney Road. It's a guilty pleasure but their lamb koftas taste amazingly good. So here's my own version! If you prefer a slightly healthier treat, you can griddle the koftas instead of frying them.

1. Heat a frying pan with 1 tablespoon of olive oil over a medium heat, then soften the onion for 3 minutes. Be careful not to let it brown. Once softened, let it cool to room temperature.

2. When the onion is cool, put it in a large mixing bowl with all the remaining ingredients for the koftas and mix thoroughly with your hands, so everything is well combined. Leave to rest for 30 minutes in the fridge so the flavours can infuse.

3. Once rested, mould the kofta mixture with your hands into small sausage-like shapes. You should get about 24. Chill the koftas in the fridge for another 30 minutes.

4. Meanwhile, make the spiced yoghurt. Mix all the ingredients in a small bowl and season with salt. Set aside until ready to serve.

5. Top and tail the cucumber and use a vegetable peeler to peel off thin slices lengthways. Once you get to the seeds, turn the cucumber onto the other side and do the same. You do not want the seeds/core. You will need to do this on all four sides.

6. Discard the core/seeds and place the ribbons in a mixing bowl. Squeeze the lemon juice over the cucumber and season with salt. Mix together and set aside until ready to serve.

7. When the koftas have chilled, heat two large frying pans on a medium heat, each with 2 tablespoons of olive oil. Fry the koftas for 4–5 minutes on each side, until crisp and browned, adding another tablespoon of olive oil if the pan looks dry. To check they are cooked, stab through the middle with a knife to make sure the mince is not pink. They should take 8–10 minutes in total. Remove from the pan and drain on kitchen paper to remove excess oil. (If using just one pan, fry in batches and keep the cooked koftas warm in a low oven.)

8. When ready to serve, toast the pine nuts in a dry frying pan over a low heat for 2 minutes until beginning to brown. Warm the pittas in the oven or in a toaster. Serve four koftas per person, along with pitta, spiced yoghurt and cucumber ribbons, and garnish with crumbled feta and the toasted pine nuts.

DIPPY DOUGHNUTS

MAKES 16

FOR THE DOUGHNUTS
250g strong white flour,
　　plus extra for dusting
Pinch of salt
1 tsp dried yeast
160g caster sugar
40g butter, softened
150ml warm milk
Vegetable oil, for frying

FOR THE CARAMEL SAUCE
250g caster sugar
150ml double cream
50g unsalted butter

FOR THE CHOCOLATE DIPPING SAUCE
100g dark chocolate, broken
　　into pieces
100ml double cream
1 tbsp vanilla paste
2 tbsp honey

EQUIPMENT
Deep-fat fryer (or a
　　deep saucepan and
　　oil thermometer)

This would be Homer Simpson's idea of heaven! For an extra-special finish, you can roll the doughnuts in flavoured sugar, such as cinnamon or vanilla, which can be bought in jars from larger supermarkets (look in the baking aisle), or simply mix up your own.

1　Combine the flour, salt, yeast and 60g of the sugar in a mixing bowl. Mix in the soft butter, then slowly stir in the warm milk until it becomes a dough.

2　Turn out the dough onto a floured work surface and knead for about 5 minutes until smooth and elastic. Lightly oil a bowl and place the dough in it, then cover with cling film, lay a tea towel on top and leave to stand for 2 hours.

3　After 2 hours, roll the dough into a 20cm-long log, halve it and cut each half into eight equal pieces (giving 16 in total). Roll each piece into a ball, poke your finger through it if you like your doughnuts with holes, and flatten slightly. Place onto a baking tray to stand for 20 minutes, covered loosely with cling film.

4　To make the caramel sauce, heat the sugar and 5 tablespoons of water in a saucepan over a medium–high heat, swirling the pan now and again until the sugar has dissolved. It is important not to stir as this will cause the sugar to crystallise, which will ruin your caramel. Turn up the heat and boil for about 5 minutes, still without stirring, until you have a rich golden caramel. Remove from the heat and stir in the cream and butter. Be careful as the caramel will be very hot and may spit. Set aside until ready to serve.

5　Preheat a deep-fat fryer to 160°C (or use a deep, heavy-based saucepan and an oil thermometer to regulate the temperature) and spread the remaining caster sugar on a flat plate or board. Fry the doughnuts in batches of about four, for 3–4 minutes until golden. Turn regularly so they cook evenly. Remove using a slotted spoon and drain on kitchen paper.

6　While still hot, roll the doughnuts in the remaining caster sugar, then leave to cool for 2 minutes.

7　To make the chocolate sauce, melt all the ingredients in a pan on a medium heat. When the mixture thickens, remove from the heat and pour into ramekins or little pots to serve.

8　When ready to serve, gently reheat the caramel sauce and place in ramekins or pots. Serve the doughnuts with both dips alongside.

CINNAMON APPLE RINGS WITH CARAMEL SAUCE & VANILLA CREAM

SERVES 4–6

FOR THE APPLES
6 Granny Smith apples,
    peeled and cored but
    kept whole
150g plain flour
¼ tsp baking powder
Pinch of salt
250g natural yoghurt
1 egg, beaten
200g golden caster sugar
1 tbsp ground cinnamon
Vegetable oil, for frying

FOR THE VANILLA CREAM
250ml double cream
1 tbsp vanilla paste
2 tbsp icing sugar

FOR THE CARAMEL SAUCE
250g caster sugar
150ml double cream
50g unsalted butter

EQUIPMENT
Deep-fat fryer (or a deep,
    wide saucepan)

Okay, so these are a bit of an indulgence, but I like to pretend they count towards one of your 5-a-day! I've used yoghurt in the batter, which gives a nice, thick consistency and helps takes the edge off the sweetness. Granny Smiths are the best apples here, because they are firm enough to keep their shape during frying; most other apples will collapse.

1. First make the caramel sauce. Heat the sugar and 5 tablespoons of water in a saucepan over a medium–high heat, swirling the pan now and again until the sugar has dissolved. It is important not to stir as this will cause the sugar to crystallise, which will ruin your caramel. Increase the heat and boil for about 5 minutes, still without stirring, until you have a rich golden caramel. Remove from the heat and stir in the cream and butter. Be careful as the caramel will be very hot and may spit. Set aside until ready to serve.

2. To make the vanilla cream, put the cream, vanilla paste and icing sugar into a bowl and whisk until it forms medium-stiff peaks. Place in a serving bowl and chill until needed.

3. In a bowl, mix the flour, baking powder and salt. In another bowl, whisk together the yoghurt and egg until combined, then pour them into the flour mixture, whisking as you go. Gradually whisk in 50ml of water until you have a thick batter. Let it rest for 10 minutes.

4. Meanwhile, put the golden caster sugar and cinnamon in a bowl and mix together well. Cut the apples into 1cm rings.

5. Preheat a deep-fat fryer to 190°C. If don't have a deep-fat fryer, you can shallow-fry in a wide, deep saucepan with 2cm of oil.

6. When the batter has rested, dip the apple rings in it, shake off the excess and fry in batches of two for 1–2 minutes on each side until golden and crisp. You need to flip them and cook on both sides, regardless of whether you are using a saucepan or a deep-fat fryer. Remove using a slotted spoon and rest them on kitchen paper, then dip into the cinnamon sugar, making sure you coat both sides. Shake off the excess sugar and set aside, until ready to serve. You can keep the cooked ones warm in an oven on a low heat while you fry the rest.

7. When ready to serve, gently reheat the caramel sauce and place in a bowl to serve alongside the apple rings and vanilla cream.

STEAMING, SIMMERING & POACHING

STEAMING, SIMMERING AND POACHING ARE CONSIDERED THE HEALTHIER

cooking techniques as they tend to use water (or stock) rather than oil or fat, so if you're watching your waistline (like I'm constantly doing!) then start right here.

When steaming, it's easiest to use a steaming basket, which fits inside the pan with its lid on, but you can use a colander set over a shallow pan of simmering water. Always line the basket or colander with parchment paper though, as I've made the mistake of not doing this in the past and half my food got stuck in the steamer.

Poaching eggs is something many people are scared of, but actually it's easy when you know how. I've included a couple of good poaching tips along with my recipes for Eggs Benedict and Eggs Royale, either of which will set you up for the day. Or if you're feeling spicy, my take on Mexican eggs will certainly give a kick to your breakfast or brunch, and is also a pretty good hangover cure... or so I'm told by my friends!

You'll find a pasta recipe in this chapter, and I've also included an easy recipe for gnocchi, which are surprisingly simple to make from scratch and, once shaped, are so much quicker to cook than pasta. And because they bob to the top of the pan when cooked, you can see instantly when they're ready.

So not only is this section ideal for the health-conscious, but since most of the recipes are also very quick and easy, these are great techniques to turn to when you're in a hurry and looking for a tasty dinner, fast!

MEXICAN-STYLE EGGS

SERVES 4

FOR THE EGGS

1 tbsp olive oil
½ red onion, finely chopped
1 red pepper, deseeded and cut into 1cm dice
75g chorizo, skin removed and cut into 1cm dice
1 tbsp jalapeños (from a jar), roughly chopped
1 x 400g tin of chopped tomatoes
¼ tsp paprika
Few drops of Tabasco sauce (optional)
1 x 215g tin of refried beans
4 free-range eggs
Salt and pepper

TO SERVE

4 flour tortillas
40g Cheddar cheese, grated
2 tbsp freshly chopped coriander
1 red chilli, finely sliced (optional)
60g soured cream (optional)

This bold breakfast or brunch will certainly give you the fire you need to start the day, and is also a great hangover cure. Adjust the spiciness to your taste, adding more Tabasco if you like it really hot.

1. Heat the olive oil in a large (30cm diameter) sauté pan (with a lid) over a low-medium heat and gently soften the onion. After 2 minutes, add the red pepper and cook for a further 3 minutes.

2. Add the chorizo and cook for another 2–3 minutes until it releases its natural oils. Add the jalapeños and cook for another 2 minutes.

3. Next add the tomatoes, paprika and Tabasco (if using) and stir everything together. Bring to the boil, then simmer for 4 minutes on a medium heat.

4. When the tomatoes have thickened slightly, add the refried beans, season with salt and pepper and cook for a further 2 minutes. Using a spoon, make four little wells spaced apart from each other in the mixture and crack an egg into each one.

5. Turn up the heat, put a lid on the pan and cook for 4–5 minutes until the whites have set. You don't want to overcook the eggs, or the yolks will not be runny. Season the eggs with a little salt and a grind of black pepper.

6. When you are ready to serve, warm the tortillas on a griddle, for 10–15 seconds on each side, then spoon one egg on top of each. Finish with grated cheese and coriander, plus chilli and soured cream (if using). The sauce is best served hot from the pan.

VARIATION

To make **Eggs Royale**, replace the Serrano ham with 200g of smoked salmon. Follow the recipe opposite throughout, but serve with 50g of salmon per person.

EGGS BENEDICT

Here are two brilliant breakfasts – Eggs Benedict (with ham) and Eggs Royale (with smoked salmon, see opposite), both with poached eggs and creamy hollandaise sauce. I like to use duck eggs in my sauce as it adds an extra bit of luxury and makes it richer in flavour. But you can of course use normal hens' eggs if you can't source duck eggs.

SERVES 4

8 eggs
1 tbsp white wine vinegar
4 English muffins
Butter, for spreading
8 slices of Serrano ham
2 tbsp finely chopped
   chives
Salt and pepper

FOR THE DUCK EGG HOLLANDAISE

200g unsalted butter
75ml white wine vinegar
1 bay leaf
1 tsp black peppercorns
3 duck egg yolks
Squeeze of lemon juice

1 First clarify the butter for the hollandaise. In a saucepan on a low heat, gently melt the butter. Simmer for 2–3 minutes until a white foam comes to the surface and the butter has stopped spluttering. Using a slotted spoon, skim the white foam from the surface and discard. Carefully pour the clear butter into a jug, leaving the white solids at the bottom of the pan; these solids can also be discarded. The clear liquid is the clarified butter, which keeps well in the fridge for 3–6 months.

2 To make the hollandaise sauce, put the vinegar, bay leaf and peppercorns in a saucepan and boil over a medium–high heat until the vinegar has reduced by two-thirds: you want to end up with 2 tablespoons. Pass through a fine sieve and set aside.

3 Place a heatproof bowl over a saucepan of simmering water and add the duck egg yolks, reduced vinegar and a pinch of salt, and whisk until it thickens and becomes a little paler.

4 In a slow, steady stream, and whisking all the time, add the clarified butter to the bowl. Don't add it too quickly, or the sauce may split. (Quickly remove the bowl from the saucepan if you think it is going to split: cook it gently.) Once all the butter is added, continue cooking the sauce until it thickens. Keep whisking at all times.

5 Remove the sauce from the heat and add a squeeze of lemon juice and a good grind of pepper, and taste to see if more salt is needed. Keep it warm until ready to serve. If the sauce is a little too thick, add a splash of water to loosen it.

6 When you are ready to eat, bring a large saucepan of salted water to the boil and add the tablespoon of vinegar.

7 Crack the first batch of eggs (two or three) into ramekins (one egg per ramekin). Holding the ramekins close to the water, gently tip the egg in and poach for 1–2 minutes until the egg sets. Remove using a slotted spoon. Continue in batches until all the eggs are poached.

8 Split each muffin in half, toast and butter it. Place two slices of Serrano ham and two eggs per person on top of the muffins; season with salt and pepper. Spoon over the hollandaise and garnish with chives. Serve straightaway.

PRAWN & PORK DUMPLINGS

MAKES 30

150g minced pork
150g raw shelled tiger
    prawns, cut into
    5mm dice
3 spring onions, finely
    chopped
1 garlic clove, crushed
2cm piece of ginger, peeled
    and grated
1 tbsp mirin or rice wine
    vinegar
1 tbsp sesame oil
1 tbsp soy sauce
1 packet of wonton
    wrappers
Sweet chilli sauce, to serve

EQUIPMENT
Steamer, preferably
    bamboo

When I have friends over for dinner, I often do 'themed' nights. Sometimes I bite off more than I can chew by making lots of different dishes, but it gives me a chance to try all sorts of new recipes. I first made these dumplings for a Chinese-themed night and they went down a storm. You can steam them as described or deep-fry them if you prefer (see Tip); they are just as awesome either way. For the wonton wrappers, you may need to visit a Chinese or Asian supermarket.

1. In a large mixing bowl, combine the pork mince, prawns, spring onions, garlic, ginger, mirin, sesame oil and soy sauce. Put in the fridge to marinate for 30 minutes.

2. When marinated, spoon 1 teaspoon of the mixture into the centre of each wonton wrapper.

3. To seal the wrappers, use a pastry brush to brush around the outside with cold water, bring all the corners to the middle and scrunch together, twisting slightly.

4. Once all the wontons have been made you can chill them in the fridge for a few hours until ready to cook, or steam them straightaway.

5. To cook, line the steamer with parchment paper and steam the dumplings for 5–6 minutes. Serve straightaway with sweet chilli sauce for dipping.

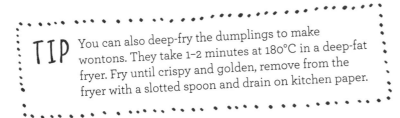

TIP You can also deep-fry the dumplings to make wontons. They take 1–2 minutes at 180°C in a deep-fat fryer. Fry until crispy and golden, remove from the fryer with a slotted spoon and drain on kitchen paper.

POACHED PEARS WITH BLUE CHEESE & BITTER LEAVES

People usually think of poached pears as a dessert, but they are also great as a starter – this salad is a perfect mix of sweet and savoury, with lots of different textures. (But if you *are* in a sweet mood, you can poach the pears in the same way and serve minus the salad and cheese, with a big dollop of ice cream instead.)

SERVES 4 AS A STARTER

FOR THE BLUE CHEESE SALAD

80g mixed bitter leaves (frisée/rocket/radicchio)
200g blue cheese, such as Roquefort or Stilton
75g walnuts, toasted and roughly chopped

FOR THE POACHED PEARS

375ml red wine (Cabernet Sauvignon)
200g golden caster sugar
1 cinnamon stick
4 Concorde or Conference pears, peeled and bottoms trimmed flat

FOR THE DRESSING

2 tbsp olive oil
2 tbsp walnut oil
2 tbsp red wine vinegar
Salt

1. First, poach the pears. Place the wine, sugar and cinnamon stick into a saucepan with 250ml of water. Stand the pears in the pan and bring to the boil. Reduce the heat and simmer with the lid on for 20 minutes, until the pears are tender but firm.

2. Remove from the pan using a slotted spoon and allow them to cool. When cool, split the pears into sixths lengthways, removing and discarding the core and stalk.

3. To prepare the dressing, place all the ingredients in a jam jar and shake them so they all mix together, or whisk them in a small bowl. Season with a pinch of salt.

4. Place the bitter leaves into a mixing bowl and pour over the dressing, reserving 2 tablespoons. Using your hands, gently toss the leaves so everything is dressed.

5. Arrange a quarter of the leaves on each plate and lay six pear slices randomly on top of them. Scatter with crumbled blue cheese and walnuts, and finish with the half a tablespoon of reserved dressing for each plate.

FEE FI PHO YUM! (CHICKEN PHO)

SERVES 4

FOR THE BROTH

1 medium chicken, jointed
(see overleaf; you need
breasts, wings and
carcass only)
4 cloves
1 cinnamon stick
1 tbsp coriander seeds
3 cardamom pods
1 star anise
1 tbsp Szechuan
peppercorns
1 large onion, left unpeeled
7.5cm piece of ginger, left
unpeeled
3 tbsp fish sauce, plus extra
for finishing
1 tbsp palm sugar
2 pak or bok choi

TO SERVE

400g ready-cooked rice
noodles
100g beansprouts
Bunch of spring onions,
finely sliced
1 red chilli, finely sliced
4 tbsp roughly chopped
coriander
3 tbsp roughly chopped
mint
1 lime, cut into wedges
(optional)

Pho is a traditional Vietnamese broth of noodles and meat. I love Vietnamese food as it's so fresh-tasting and extremely healthy. The longer you cook the broth, the more flavour it takes on, so give it a nice long time and it will become even more YUM!

1 Make sure all the skin and fat is removed from the chicken carcass. Place it into a pot along with the wings and skinless breasts and cover with 3 litres of water. Bring to the boil and simmer for 5 minutes, then drain and discard the water. This is to remove any impurities and blood. Put the chicken pieces into a clean pot (or clean out the same pot and use it again).

2 Toast all the dried spices for the broth in a dry frying pan over a low heat for 2 minutes until you can smell them, then add to the chicken pot.

3 Over a medium–hot naked flame or on a griddle pan on a hot hob, char the onion and ginger (both with skin on) until heavily charred and black. This is key to an authentic flavour. Let them cool slightly, then peel the onion and chop in half. Also peel the ginger. Add them to the pot, along with the fish sauce and palm sugar.

4 Top up with 3 litres of water and bring to the boil. Once it has boiled, reduce the heat and cover with a lid. Simmer for 2–2½ hours. The longer you cook the broth, the more intense a flavour you will get. Skim the fat and impurities from the surface every 30 minutes.

5 Once the broth is ready, remove the chicken pieces using tongs. Discard the onions, ginger and chicken carcass and strain the broth into another pot using a colander, discarding the spices.

6 Shred the chicken breast using a knife and pick the meat from the wings, discarding the skin and bones. Return all the meat to the broth.

7 Now add the pak or bok choi and simmer for 3–4 minutes until tender. Check the seasoning as you may need to add a little more fish sauce.

8 To serve, divide the noodles and beansprouts between four bowls, then ladle the broth and chicken over the top. Garnish with spring onions, chilli, coriander and mint, and a lime wedge if you like. Serve hot.

JOINT YOUR CHICKEN →

1

Using a sharp knife, cut through the skin around one leg to loosen it up and let you ease the leg away from the body. Then cut around the leg again, deeper this time until you reach the joint.

TIP Where the thigh joins the backbone there is a fleshy piece of meat called the 'oyster'; make sure to release this on each side when taking the legs off until it comes free from the bird.

4

Turn the chicken on its side and cut along the joint. Use your hands to break the joint, then use your knife to cut the wing until it comes free from the bird. Repeat for the other wing and set both wings aside for the pho.

2

Turn the chicken on its side and cut along the joint. Break the joint with your hands, then use your knife to cut off the leg. Repeat for the other leg and set both legs aside. You can freeze them or use them for another dish, as they are not required for the pho.

3

Using a sharp knife, cut through the skin around each wing and follow through until you reach the joint.

5

Run your knife along one side of the backbone from one end to the other, and carefully follow the bone downwards, gently cutting to remove the breast. Repeat for the other breast, then remove the skin from both breasts and discard it.

6

Trim the excess skin from the carcass and discard it, keeping the carcass for the stock.

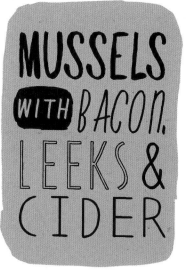

MUSSELS WITH BACON, LEEKS & CIDER

I used to work in Covent Garden and would often go with work mates to a restaurant called Belgo, which serves *moules-frites* (mussels and chips). Now that I no longer work there, I often crave mussels, as I'm a big fan. I've given you two options here: the main recipe has cider and bacon, which I like to think of as British mussels, and the variation below uses white wine and garlic, which is the classic French combination.

SERVES 2

1kg fresh mussels
100g smoked bacon
   lardons
1 leek, white parts only,
   finely sliced
1 celery stick, finely sliced
1 banana or Echalion
   shallot, finely sliced
2 garlic cloves, peeled
200ml dry cider
Juice of ½ lemon
150ml crème fraîche
2 tbsp finely chopped
   chervil or tarragon
2 tbsp finely chopped
   parsley
Olive oil
Salt and pepper

1 Put the mussels into a colander and run them under cold water. You want to clean them and discard any bad ones. To tell if a mussel is bad, tap it on the side of the colander – if it doesn't close, discard it. To clean, pull off the beard (stringy bit) and remove any barnacles growing on the outside using a small paring knife. Once cleaned, put into a bowl until ready to use.

2 In a large cooking pot or saucepan with a lid, heat a good glug of olive oil and gently fry the bacon lardons over a medium heat for a few minutes until they start to colour. When they begin to crisp up, add the leek, celery and shallot and cook for 2–3 minutes until the leeks and shallots are soft but not brown. Now crush the garlic into the pan and cook for a further 2–3 minutes until the leeks are translucent.

3 Pour the cider into the pan and bring to the boil, then simmer for 3 minutes to cook off the alcohol.

4 Add the mussels, cover the pan with a lid and let them steam for 4–5 minutes until they have all opened. Holding the lid clamped shut, give the pan a shake every now and then so they all cook.

5 Once the mussels have all opened (discard any that don't), add the lemon juice and crème fraîche and simmer for another minute. Add the fresh herbs and season with just a little salt (as the bacon and mussels are already salty) and a good crack of pepper. Serve with crusty bread.

VARIATION

For **Mussels with White Wine and Garlic**, follow the recipe as above, but omit the bacon and leek, double the quantity of shallots and garlic cloves, and substitute the cider with 150ml white wine and the crème fraîche with 150ml double cream. First, clean the mussels as above. Then, soften the shallots and celery as above, for 2–3 minutes, add the garlic and cook for another 2–3 minutes until the shallots are translucent. At this point add the wine. Follow the method above for the rest of the recipe.

ROCKET & ALMOND PESTO PASTA

SERVES 4

400g farfalle pasta, or
   shape of choice
50g whole almonds, skin on
50g rocket, plus extra for
   serving
50g Parmesan cheese,
   finely grated, plus extra
   shavings for serving
Juice of 1 lemon
2 garlic cloves, crushed
3 basil sprigs
100ml olive oil, plus extra
   for drizzling
Salt and pepper

I wrote this recipe for my mum, who is a big fan of pesto. The traditional version uses pine nuts, but I've given it a twist by swapping in my favourite nuts: almonds. Or you can use walnuts if you like. In the summer, the rocket can be switched for sorrel, which adds a lovely lemony zing. Look for it at a farmers' market.

1 Bring a large saucepan of water to boiling point and season with salt. Add the pasta and a drizzle of olive oil and cook according to the packet instructions.

2 In a dry frying pan on a low heat, lightly toast the almonds for 2 minutes. Transfer to a food processor.

3 Add all the remaining ingredients and blitz to a smooth purée. If you don't have a food processor, you can grind the ingredients with a pestle and mortar. Season with salt and pepper, spoon into a jar or bowl and set aside until ready to serve.

4 When the pasta is cooked, drain and return it to the hot saucepan. Add 4–5 tablespoons of the pesto and mix well. Serve hot with a handful of rocket, a few shavings of Parmesan and a drizzle of olive oil.

5 Put any remaining pesto in a jar with a little oil on top to prevent discolouration. It will keep for 3–4 days in the fridge.

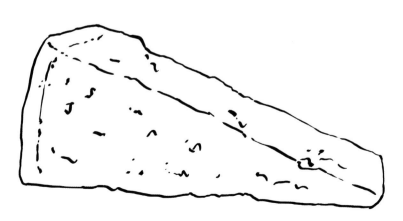

SPINACH & RICOTTA GNOCCHI *WITH* WALNUTS

SERVES 4

FOR THE GNOCCHI
250g fresh spinach
250g ricotta, strained of any liquid
125g Parmesan cheese, finely grated
2 egg yolks, beaten
1 garlic clove, crushed
½ nutmeg, finely grated
175g '00' white flour (pasta flour), plus extra for shaping the gnocchi
Salt and pepper

FOR THE SAGE BEURRE NOISETTE
100g unsalted butter
15 sage leaves, roughly torn

TO SERVE
20g rocket
Juice of ½ lemon
2 tbsp olive oil
50g walnuts, roughly chopped and toasted
Shavings of Parmesan cheese

The first time I made gnocchi was at a cooking school called Mamma Agata's, on Italy's Amalfi coast. I was surprised at how easy it was to make, but if I hadn't done it there that day, it's something I would probably have been too scared to try. So give it a go yourself – it's very simple and will definitely impress your guests.

1. Put a kettle on to boil. Place the spinach in a large heatproof bowl, pour over the boiling water from the kettle, and leave to blanch for 1–2 minutes until wilted.

2. Strain the spinach in a colander, tip it into the centre of a clean tea towel or muslin cloth and wring out excess water over the sink. Place on a chopping board and finely chop.

3. Put the chopped spinach in a large bowl and mix with the remaining ingredients, excluding the flour. Then gradually add the flour, mixing to combine, and season with salt and pepper. Cover with cling film and chill for 30 minutes.

4. Once chilled, remove the spinach mixture from the fridge. Add a good handful of '00' flour to a roasting tin. Take a teaspoonful of the mixture and roll between your palms into a small oval ball, then roll in the floured tray and set aside on a plate. Continue until the spinach mixture is used up.

5. Bring a large pot of salted water to the boil and, in two batches, cook the gnocchi. When they have all risen to the top, cook for 1 minute more, then remove using a slotted spoon. Keep warm and cook the second batch.

6. Meanwhile, make the beurre noisette. In a large frying pan, melt the butter and sage leaves for 1–2 minutes until the butter is dark brown or hazelnut in colour. Remove from the heat.

7. When the gnocchi are cooked, add them to the beurre noisette and toss so everything is well coated.

8. In a small bowl, mix the rocket and lemon juice and drizzle with olive oil.

9. Spoon the gnocchi into bowls and top with a handful of the dressed rocket, some walnut pieces and shavings of Parmesan.

MINI STICKY TOFFEE PUDS WITH CARDAMOM CUSTARD

Sticky toffee pudding with custard reminds me of school dinners... although the puddings we ate at school weren't anywhere *near* as tasty as these. And the custard was always neon-coloured and full of lumps! So, this is a school memory put right.

MAKES 6

FOR THE STICKY PUDS
100g unsalted butter, plus extra for greasing
4 tbsp golden syrup
120g golden caster sugar
2 eggs
120g plain flour
1 tsp baking powder
Pinch of salt

FOR THE CARDAMOM CUSTARD
300ml double cream
300ml whole milk
6 cardamom pods
4 egg yolks
70g caster sugar

EQUIPMENT
6 x 150ml mini pudding moulds (or more/fewer depending on size)

1. Grease the mini moulds with butter and line with a circle of baking parchment. Then drizzle 2 teaspoons of golden syrup into each one.

2. In a mixing bowl, beat together the butter and sugar until light and fluffy, then whisk in the eggs. Sift in the flour, baking powder and salt, and stir until you have a smooth batter.

3. Spoon the batter into the pudding moulds. Put a small round circle of baking parchment on top of each pudding – this traps the steam in and helps keep the pudding level when rising.

4. Cover the tops of the pudding moulds with foil, folding a small pleat into the top of each piece of foil to allow for expansion during cooking. Tie string around each mould to secure the foil.

5. Put the moulds into a large empty saucepan and add enough water to come three-quarters of the way up the side of the moulds. Remove the moulds and put the saucepan on to boil.

6. When boiling, reduce the heat so the water simmers, and place the moulds back in the water. Cook for 45–50 minutes until the puddings have cooked all the way through. To test whether they are cooked, insert a skewer through the foil of one pudding, about halfway into the sponge (don't go too far or you will reach the syrup). If the skewer comes out clean, the puddings are ready. If not, give them a little more time and then test again.

CONTINUES

CONTINUED

7 Meanwhile, make the custard. Pour the double cream and milk into a saucepan. Split the cardamom pods and add the seeds and pods to the pan. Heat on a medium temperature until it reaches 80°C on a cooking thermometer (if you have one) or just starts to boil. Then remove from the heat and let it infuse for 30 minutes.

8 While the cream mixture is infusing, beat the egg yolks with the sugar in a mixing bowl until pale and fluffy. Once infused, strain the cream/milk mixture through a fine sieve into a new saucepan. Place it back on the heat and bring back to 80°C or just before boiling. Then slowly and gradually pour it into the bowl with the eggs, whisking all the time. You must keep whisking, or the eggs will scramble.

9 When everything is combined, return it to the saucepan on a medium heat and cook until it reaches 80°C or is just before boiling again, stirring continuously with a wooden spoon. When it reaches this point, the custard mixture will be thick enough to coat the back of the spoon. Remove from the heat.

10 When the puddings are cooked, remove the moulds from the saucepan, take off the string and foil, flip upside down and tap out. Serve hot, with the custard.

LAVENDER CRÈME BRÛLÉE with BLACKBERRY COMPOTE

The first time I used lavender in cooking was on *MasterChef* when I was making a dessert for a group of Italian artists. It was a success and they really liked the flavour. Since then, I've tried to find other ways to include lavender in desserts and this is one of my favourites. The combination of blackberries and lavender here works perfectly and gives a nice touch of English countryside to classic crème brûlée. Make sure you use *edible* lavender flowers (sometimes sold as 'herb lavender').

SERVES 4

500ml double cream
1 tbsp lavender flowers (make sure they are culinary/edible flowers)
1 tsp vanilla paste
6 egg yolks
100g caster sugar, plus 4 tbsp to finish

FOR THE COMPOTE
160g blackberries
2 tbsp caster sugar

EQUIPMENT
4 x 150ml ramekins
Blow torch (optional)

1. In a saucepan on a medium heat, bring the cream, lavender flowers and vanilla paste to boiling point, then remove from the heat and leave for 45 minutes to infuse.

2. Preheat the oven to 150°C/130°C fan/gas mark 2. In a mixing bowl, whisk together the egg yolks and 100g of caster sugar.

3. Reheat the cream until just before boiling point, then pour it over the sugar mixture and whisk for 1 minute. Strain into a measuring jug using a fine sieve (to remove all the flowers).

4. Place the four ramekins in a roasting tin and divide the mixture equally between them. Boil a kettle, then pour the boiling water into the roasting tin so it comes halfway up the outside of the ramekins.

5. Cook in the oven for 35-45 minutes until the brûlées are set. Once set, remove the tray from the oven and take the ramekins out the tray so they don't continue to cook. Allow them to cool to room temperature, then chill in the fridge until ready to serve.

6. To prepare the compote, place the ingredients in a saucepan and cook over a gentle heat for a few minutes until the fruit breaks down. Stir regularly to prevent it catching on the bottom of the pan. Set aside to keep warm until ready to serve. This can be made in advance, as it keeps in the fridge for 1-2 days, and can be gently reheated when ready to serve (or served cold).

7. When you are ready to serve, sprinkle a tablespoon of golden caster sugar over each set brûlée.

8. Using a blowtorch, heat the sugar topping until it caramelises. If you don't have a blow torch, you can do it under the grill. Make sure the grill is preheated so you can caramelise the sugar as quickly as possible, to avoid the custard base melting or continuing to cook.

9. Serve straightaway, with the warm compote in a bowl alongside, ready to be spooned on top.

3

CIDER

CO

SLOW COOKING IS ONE OF MY FAVOURITE COOKING TECHNIQUES

for two reasons: firstly, once you've got the prep out of the way, you're free to go about your business for a good few hours while your dinner simmers away in the oven. And secondly: slow cooking rewards you with meat that literally falls off the bone and melts in your mouth like angels dancing on your tongue! If only everything in life were this simple.

In this chapter I've used some cheaper cuts of meat, such as braising steak, which needs to be cooked slowly; chicken thighs, which are better value and absorb far more flavour than chicken breast; and lamb shoulder, a surprisingly economical yet tasty choice for your Sunday roast. I've also used beef cheeks, which you can get from most butchers but are often overlooked these days for more popular alternatives. I say give me beef cheek over fillet any day. When cooked for hours on end, the fibres in the cheeks break down and become far more mouth-watering and succulent than a steak could ever be.

I've included recipes for my guilty (and not-so-guilty) pleasures, such as pulled pork, chilli tacos and Korean pork belly wraps, inspired by the kind of food I tuck into with friends around east London's amazing street food vendors. You can also try my delicious recipes for confit duck and confit fennel, which when said in a French accent ('con–fee') will make you sound *very* sophisticated. They are in fact surprisingly easy to make and basically involve cooking food very slowly in fat or oil (though not like they do in terrible fast-food chains!), which keeps it tender and moist and adds amazing flavour.

Slow cooking gives you more time to relax but the finished results will make it seem like you've been slaving away all day!

CHILLI TACO CHOW DOWN

FOR THE CHILLI

750g lean beef steak mince
1 large red onion, finely
  diced
2 red sweet pointed
  peppers, deseeded and
  cut into 1cm chunks
2 garlic cloves, crushed
2 x 400g tins of chopped
  tomatoes
1 x 400g tin of kidney
  beans, rinsed
2 tbsp tomato purée
1 cinnamon stick
1 star anise
1 tsp smoked paprika
1 tsp ground cumin
1 tsp cayenne pepper
1 tsp caster sugar
1 tbsp Worcestershire
  sauce
200ml beef stock
Olive oil
Salt and pepper

TO SERVE

18 taco shells
100g Cheddar cheese,
  grated
1 iceberg lettuce, shredded
250ml soured cream
Leaves from a bunch of
  coriander, finely chopped
1 x 200g jar of jalapeño
  peppers (optional, if you
  want extra spice)

Chilli tacos remind me of a family holiday to Florida, where I tried them for the first time. I reckon it's the best way to serve chilli, although you can also serve it the traditional way with rice. This makes a brilliant dinner for when you have friends over on the weekend and it's great washed down with an ice-cold beer.

1 In a large frying pan on a medium heat, warm 1 tablespoon of olive oil, add the beef mince and cook for about 5 minutes until brown. When browned, remove from the heat and drain off the excess fat through a fine colander.

2 In a large cooking pot (with lid), heat 1 tablespoon of olive oil and cook the onion for 2–3 minutes on a low heat until soft but not brown. Add the red pepper (plus another tablespoon of olive oil if the pan seems dry) and cook for a further 3 minutes. Add the garlic and cook for 2 minutes until soft but not brown.

3 Add the chopped tomatoes, kidney beans and tomato purée and stir so everything is mixed together. Add the cinnamon stick, star anise, paprika, cumin, cayenne pepper, sugar and Worcestershire sauce and cook for 5 minutes.

4 Add the cooked mince and the stock, season with salt and pepper and bring to the boil, then reduce to the lowest heat, cover and simmer for 3½ hours, stirring every 30 minutes, so that nothing sticks to the bottom. Then remove the lid and cook for a further 30 minutes uncovered on a gentle simmer.

5 When cooked, remove the star anise and cinnamon stick and place the pot in the middle of the table so people can help themselves. Serve with taco shells (warmed according to the packet instructions), grated cheese, shredded lettuce, soured cream, coriander and jalapeños, if using.

KOREAN-STYLE PORK BELLY

SERVES 6

FOR THE PORK
2kg pork belly, rind scored
4 baby gem lettuces,
    separated into leaves,
    to serve

FOR THE MARINADE
3 tbsp Korean soy bean
    paste
4cm piece of ginger, peeled
    and finely grated
2 garlic cloves, peeled and
    finely grated
2 tbsp honey
3 tbsp groundnut oil

**FOR THE ONION AND
RADISH SALAD**
1 onion, finely sliced
1 red onion, finely sliced
5 spring onions, finely
    sliced
50g radishes, finely sliced
2 tbsp sesame seeds
4 tbsp mirin or rice wine
    vinegar
2 tbsp caster sugar
2 tbsp soy sauce
2 tsp sesame oil
1 tsp chilli flakes

I created this recipe for my best mate Ed, who says it's probably one of the most amazing pork dishes I've ever fed him! The Korean flavours come from a fermented soy bean paste known as *doenjang* – look for it in Asian supermarkets or online. The onion and radish salad has a wonderful tang, and because the onions are soaked in water they don't make your eyes stream like they would if you ate normal raw onions. The pork itself just melts in your mouth, and piling it into little lettuce wraps is a typically Korean way of serving it.

1 Use a sharp knife to make cuts in the fat all over the pork belly.

2 Mix all the marinade ingredients in a bowl, and massage into the pork, all over the flesh and into the cuts. Place the belly on a baking tray, cover with cling film and put in the fridge to marinate for 24 hours.

3 After marinating and 30 minutes before you wish to roast it, remove the pork from the fridge and take off the cling film to allow it to warm up to room temperature.

4 Preheat the oven to 170°C/150°C fan/gas mark 3.

5 Once the meat is at room temperature, cover with foil and roast the pork for 4 hours, basting every 45 minutes or so. Remove the foil for the last hour of cooking. Turn up the oven setting to 180°C/160°C fan/gas mark 4 for the last half-hour.

6 In the final 30 minutes of the cooking time, make the salad. Place the regular and red onion slices in a mixing bowl, cover with water and leave to stand for 20 minutes.

7 Drain the onions and add the spring onions, radishes and sesame seeds, and mix well. Whisk the other ingredients, then dress the salad and set aside until ready to serve.

8 When the pork is done, remove from the oven and let it rest for 15 minutes, covered with foil.

9 When ready to eat, remove the pork fat and skin, then slice the meat into 1cm-thick slices. To serve, load a couple of pork slices onto each lettuce leaf and top with the onion and radish salad.

CHICKEN TAGINE WITH JEWELLED COUSCOUS

SERVES 4

FOR THE TAGINE

8 chicken thighs (approx. 1.5kg), bone in, skin on
2 tbsp ras el hanout
2 tbsp olive oil, plus extra for frying
2 red onions, finely sliced
2 garlic cloves, crushed
1 x 400g tin of chopped tomatoes
100g green pitted olives
3 tbsp finely chopped coriander
3 tbsp finely chopped parsley
Salt and pepper

FOR THE JEWELLED COUSCOUS

200g couscous
250ml hot chicken stock
1 onion, finely diced
75g whole almonds, skin on
150g pomegranate seeds
100g ready-to-eat dried apricots, roughly chopped
Grated zest and juice of 1 lemon
3 tbsp chopped mint
3 tbsp chopped coriander
Olive oil

TO SERVE

2 tbsp roughly chopped coriander, plus handful of leaves to garnish
100g natural yoghurt

EQUIPMENT

Tagine pot (or casserole dish)

The chicken here is marinated with ras-el-hanout, an aromatic spice rub from North Africa. It's commonly available in supermarket spice sections, or easy to buy online. This recipe has converted all the non-couscous eaters in my family. Before they tried this, my grandad claimed couscous tasted like sawdust, while my Aunty Linda and my dad wouldn't even touch it. But thanks to this recipe, now they all love it. The fruits and nuts add sweetness and crunch, which works perfectly with the flavours of the chicken.

1. Using a small serrated knife, score the chicken skin, which allows the marinade flavours to get into the meat.

2. Place the chicken thighs, ras el hanout and olive oil in a mixing bowl and massage the spice mix into the chicken. Leave to marinate for 4 hours or preferably overnight.

3. If using a casserole dish rather than a traditional tagine pot, preheat the oven to 180°C/160°C fan/gas mark 4.

4. When the meat has marinated, warm a large frying pan with some olive oil over a gentle heat and brown the chicken in batches, for 3–4 minutes on each side, skin-side down first. Place into a tagine pot or casserole.

5. If there is lots of oil left in the pan, drain some off and then, in the same pan, soften the sliced onion for 3–4 minutes on a low heat. Add the garlic, tomatoes, olives, coriander and parsley and cook for a further 5 minutes.

6. Season with salt and pepper, then pour into the casserole or ovenproof tagine pot and place in the oven. The oven should be preheated for a casserole dish, but if you are using a tagine pot it's best put into a cold oven, then set it to 180°C/160°C fan/gas mark 4 (or follow the manufacturer's instructions for your particular tagine pot). Bake for 1 hour 15 minutes.

7. After this time, check the chicken is cooked through. If not, continue to cook until it is. If the sauce is a little thin, remove the lid and cook for a further 10–15 minutes until the sauce is thickened.

CONTINUES

CONTINUED

8 In the final 15 minutes of the cooking time, prepare the couscous. Place the couscous in a large mixing bowl and pour over the hot chicken stock. Cover with a plate and leave to stand for 10 minutes so the couscous becomes plump, then use a fork to fluff up the grains. Put the plate back on to keep it warm until needed.

9 Over a low heat, warm 1 tablespoon of olive oil in a frying pan, add the onion and cook for 2–3 minutes until translucent and soft, but not browned. When softened, add to the couscous.

10 Blitz the almonds in a food processor until in fine crumbs, then add to the couscous. Add the remaining ingredients to the couscous and dress with 3–4 tablespoons of olive oil and season with salt and pepper. Mix well.

11 When the tagine is ready, remove from the oven and scatter with the coriander leaves. Mix the chopped coriander into the yoghurt. Serve the tagine with the couscous and yoghurt on the side.

GRANDAD'S FAVOURITE BEEF & GUINNESS STEW with DUMPLINGS

SERVES 6

FOR THE STEW
1.2kg braising beef, trimmed of excess fat or sinew, cut into 3cm chunks
2 tbsp plain flour
440ml Guinness
2 onions, finely sliced
3 celery sticks, cut into 2cm chunks
2 carrots, peeled and cut into 2cm chunks
7 thyme sprigs
2 star anise
2 bay leaves
2 tbsp Worcestershire sauce
2 tbsp tomato purée
750ml beef stock
Vegetable or olive oil, for frying
Salt and pepper

FOR THE DUMPLINGS
60g suet
100g self-raising flour, plus extra for dusting
50g Cheddar, grated
2 tbsp finely chopped parsley
90–100ml warm water
Salt and pepper

Stew and dumplings is one of my grandad's favourite comfort foods, and when my nan was still alive, she always used to make it for him. He's a Dublin man, and as we all know, Ireland is the home of Guinness. So this recipe is for my grandad – he certainly gives it a big thumbs up!

1 Preheat the oven to 150°C/130°C fan/gas mark 2. Place the beef in a mixing bowl, sprinkle with the flour, season with salt and pepper and mix well so everything is coated. Alternatively, you can put it all in a plastic bag and shake well.

2 Heat a large frying pan with a little oil over a medium–high heat and, in batches, brown the beef for 1–2 minutes, then set aside on a plate.

3 Pour a little of the Guinness into the pan and bubble gently, using a wooden spoon to scrape up all the caramelised sediment at the bottom. Set aside to add to the casserole pot once the vegetables have been softened.

4 Place a casserole pot on a low–medium heat with a little oil, then soften the onion, celery and carrots for 5 minutes. When softened, add the thyme, star anise and bay leaves, then the beef and the juices and scrapings from the pan, plus the Worcestershire sauce and tomato purée. Simmer on a medium heat for a further 5 minutes.

5 Add the rest of the Guinness and bring to the boil. Pour in the stock, bring back to the boil and cook for 5 minutes. Season with pepper and a little salt, cover with a lid and cook in the oven for 3½ hours.

6 Meanwhile, make the dumplings. In a bowl, mix the suet, flour, cheese and parsley, and season with salt and pepper. Mix in the warm water little by little, mixing it in until you have a firm dough.

7 Lightly dust the work surface with a little flour. Divide the dough into eight pieces, and roll into balls.

8 In the last 20 minutes of the stew's cooking time, add the dumplings, making sure they are dunked so they are three-quarters covered by the stew.

9 When the stew is ready, remove from the oven and serve straightaway.

CONFIT DUCK SALAD

SERVES 4

FOR THE CONFIT DUCK
4 duck legs (approx. 200g
    each)
60g Maldon sea salt
Leaves from 4 thyme sprigs
750ml duck fat
Pepper

FOR THE POMEGRANATE
SALAD
2 heads of chicory (red or
    white), leaves separated
1 x 110g packet of rocket
50g radishes (breakfast),
    topped/tailed and
    quartered
100g pomegranate seeds
2 tbsp freshly sliced mint
Grated zest of ½ orange
Olive oil
Salt

FOR THE DRESSING
3 tbsp sherry vinegar
6 tbsp olive oil
1 tbsp honey
1 tbsp wholegrain mustard
Salt

Confit is a way of cooking something really slowly and immersed in fat or oil, so it ends up unbelievably tender and with amazing flavour! Doing duck this way helps to keep the flesh super-moist and the finished meat just falls off the bone. It's a great idea to strain the duck fat after cooking, and keep it in a jar to re-use, as it will have all that delicious duck flavour locked inside. You can use it to cook the ultimate Sunday roasties!

1. Put the duck legs in a bowl. Rub with the salt, season with pepper and scatter with the thyme leaves. Allow to marinate for 2 hours in the fridge.

2. When marinated, rinse the duck well under cold water and pat dry with kitchen paper, to remove any excess moisture.

3. Preheat the oven to 150°C/130°C fan/gas mark 2. Warm the duck fat in a saucepan over a low heat, until just melted.

4. Lay the duck legs in a roasting dish and cover with the melted duck fat. Cook in the oven for 2½ hours, turning every hour so they cook evenly. Once cooked, remove the legs from the fat. (You can keep the fat in a jar and use for amazing roast potatoes at a later date.)

5. When cooled slightly, pick the meat from the duck legs and set aside, covered with foil to keep warm until ready to serve.

6. Meanwhile, prepare the pomegranate salad. Heat a large griddle pan on a very hot hob. In a large mixing bowl, drizzle the chicory leaves with olive oil and season with salt, then griddle the chicory for about 20 seconds on each side, until charred. Remove from the pan and set aside until required.

7. For the dressing, mix the sherry vinegar, olive oil, honey and mustard in a small bowl and whisk well. Season with salt and set aside until ready to serve.

8. When you are ready to serve, arrange the rocket leaves, radishes and chicory on a large platter, and scatter the picked duck meat, pomegranate seeds and mint leaves over the top. Dress with the vinaigrette and finish with the orange zest.

SLOW-ROASTED LAMB with BUTTER BEANS & SALSA VERDE

SERVES 4–6

FOR THE LAMB AND BEANS

2.5kg lamb shoulder
4 garlic cloves, peeled and halved
2 rosemary sprigs
2 red onions, peeled and quartered
2 carrots, peeled and cut into chunks
2 celery sticks, cut into chunks
100ml white wine
3 x 400g tins of butter beans, drained
Olive oil
Salt and pepper

FOR THE SALSA VERDE

Juice of 1 lemon
100ml olive oil
1 garlic clove, crushed
½ red onion, roughly diced
1 tsp Dijon mustard
15g fresh parsley, leaves and stalks roughly chopped
10g fresh basil, leaves and stalks roughly chopped
15g fresh dill, leaves and stalks roughly chopped
15g fresh mint (leaves only), roughly chopped
6 anchovies
1 tbsp capers

I like to imagine that heaven will be filled with amazing foodie smells. And nothing is more heavenly than the smell of lamb roasting slowly in the oven on a Sunday afternoon. For a roast with a difference, why not try giving it a Mediterranean twist, like this?

1 Preheat the oven to 160°C/140°C fan/gas mark 3.

2 Use a small paring knife to make eight insertions into the lamb shoulder. In each hole, put half a clove of garlic and a small sprig of rosemary.

3 Put the onion, carrots and celery in a large roasting tin and place the lamb shoulder on top. Drizzle it with olive oil and season with salt and pepper. Pour the wine and 200ml of water into the roasting tin, cover with foil and cook in the oven for 2 hours 15 minutes.

4 After this time, remove the foil, add the butter beans and cook for a further 45 minutes.

5 Meanwhile, make the salsa verde. Place all the ingredients into a food processor and blend into a fine purée. Season with salt and pepper and set aside until ready to serve.

6 When the lamb is cooked, remove from the oven and leave to rest for 10–15 minutes before carving. Serve with the butter beans, vegetables and salsa verde.

AMERICAN SOUL HAM WITH CHEESY GRITS & GREENS

**SERVES 6
(WITH LEFTOVERS)**

FOR THE HAM
2kg unsmoked raw ham or
    gammon joint
1 tbsp Maldon sea salt
2 bay leaves
20 cloves

FOR THE GLAZE
2 tbsp Dijon mustard
4 tbsp honey
2 tbsp light brown sugar
Salt and pepper

FOR THE GREENS
400g spring greens, stalks
    removed, leaves sliced
    2.5cm thick
1 tsp chilli flakes
2 garlic cloves, skin on,
    lightly squashed/crushed
2 tbsp malt vinegar
3 tbsp light brown sugar

FOR THE GRITS
250ml whole milk
300g polenta
75g butter
50g Cheddar cheese,
    grated

This American-style recipe was actually inspired by a great meal I had in London, when I tried grits and collard greens for the first time. WOW, they were AMAZING!!! Both dishes are absolute classics in the American Deep South. Grits are made from thick, creamy ground maize, while collard greens are part of the cabbage family, but as it's tricky to buy authentic grits and collard greens in the UK, I've used polenta and spring greens, which are the nearest alternatives. They make fantastic sides for this tender and juicy glazed ham. Remember to cook the greens in the ham stock to pack in loads of flavour, and feel free to spice them up with more dried chilli flakes and even hot sauce, if you like things fiery.

1. Place the ham into a large lidded cooking pot, cover with water and add the salt and bay leaves. Bring to the boil, then leave to simmer with the lid on for up to 2 hours. Check it after 1 hour 30 minutes by inserting the tip of a knife into the meat – if it feels tender it has had enough time. You may need to check the water levels and top up if required.

2. When cooked, remove the ham, retaining the cooking liquid in the pot but discarding the bay leaves. Set the ham aside to cool.

3. Now, prepare the greens. Add the greens, chilli flakes, garlic, vinegar and sugar to the pot with the ham cooking liquor in it and bring to the boil. You may need to add a little extra water to cover. Once at boiling point, turn down to the lowest heat, put on the lid and leave to simmer for 1 hour 30 minutes.

4. Meanwhile, preheat the oven to 180°C/160°C fan/gas mark 4.

5. When the ham has cooled for about 15 minutes, remove the skin but leave on the fat. With a small, sharp knife, score a large criss-cross pattern all over the fat. Stud the ham with the cloves at the point of each diamond.

6. Mix the glaze ingredients in a small bowl and whisk in 4 tablespoons of water. Season with salt and pepper.

CONTINUES

CONTINUED

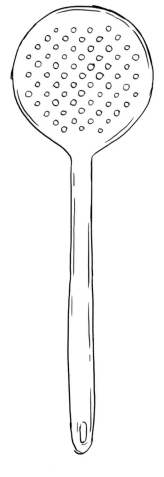

7. Line a roasting tin with kitchen foil or baking parchment (to stop the glaze burning), add the ham and pour half of the glaze over the ham, coating it evenly. Reserve the other half of the glaze for basting. Add water to the roasting tin (1cm deep) to stop it from drying out and burning. Cook in the oven for 45 minutes. Check the ham every 20 minutes, and if it seems dry, brush with more of the reserved glazed mixture to stop it drying out and burning.

8. Once the ham is cooked, remove from the oven and leave to rest on a board or plate for 10–15 minutes, covered with foil to keep in the heat.

9. When the greens are done, remove the garlic, then drain, squeezing out all the excess water in the colander. Season with pepper and then taste them, adding salt only if required. It's important to taste first as the ham liquor can be quite salty. Keep the greens warm until ready to serve.

10. Finally, make the grits. Bring the milk and 1.25 litres of water to the boil in a large saucepan over a medium–high heat, then add the polenta. Reduce the temperature to low and constantly whisk as it will thicken very quickly. Cook for 3–5 minutes, then remove from the heat and whisk in the butter and cheese. Season with salt and pepper and serve hot.

11. When you are ready to serve, remove the cloves from the ham and cut into 1–2cm slices. Serve the greens and grits on the side.

CONFIT FENNEL LINGUINE

'Confit' means cooking an ingredient slowly and immersed in fat or oil, until it becomes really tender and delicious. It's most commonly done with meat (see Confit Duck Salad on page 80) but fennel is also amazing cooked this way. I first did it on *MasterChef*, which meant practising the dish loads in advance, so I had piles of fennel confit left over. Not wanting to waste it, I tried running it through some linguine and this simple but sophisticated pasta recipe was born. You can also add freshly picked crabmeat if you want to pimp it up a bit more.

SERVES 4

4 fennel bulbs
1 garlic clove, skin on and squashed/crushed
1 tsp fennel seeds
4 strips of lemon zest
About 500ml olive oil
400g linguine
4 spring onions, finely sliced
1 red chilli, deseeded and finely sliced
2 tbsp finely sliced basil
Parmesan shavings (optional)
Salt and pepper

1. Top and tail the fennel bulbs, then remove the outer layers and discard them. Cut each fennel bulb vertically in half, then remove the core – this will be a triangular shape at the bottom of the bulb. Divide each bulb into sixths, so that you have 24 wedges in total.

2. Place the fennel wedges in a deep sauté pan along with the garlic, fennel seeds, lemon zest and a pinch of salt. Cover with the olive oil (you may need more depending on the size of your pan) and cook the fennel on a very low heat, so it simmers rather than fries, until tender. This should take 30–35 minutes. Using a slotted spoon, remove the fennel from the oil (retaining the oil for later) and drain on kitchen paper. Keep warm until ready to serve.

3. Bring a large saucepan of salted water to the boil and add the linguine. Cook according to the packet instructions. When ready, drain and return it to the pan.

4. Add the confit fennel to the linguine, then add the spring onions, chilli and basil. Dress with 4–5 tablespoons of the reserved cooking oil. Serve with Parmesan shavings (optional) and season with salt and pepper.

TIP You can pass the remaining oil from the confit through a fine sieve and put it into a clean jar or bottle. It will have an infused fennel flavour, so is good for dressing salads and fish.

SPANISH CHORIZO & CHICKPEA STEW

SERVES 6

2 tbsp olive oil, plus extra
   for drizzling
1 large onion, finely diced
1 red pepper, deseeded and
   cut into 1cm chunks
1 yellow pepper, deseeded
   and cut into 1cm chunks
2 garlic cloves, finely
   chopped or crushed
2 bay leaves
250g cooking chorizo, skin
   removed and cut into
   1cm slices
½ tsp cayenne pepper
1 tsp smoked paprika
2 x 400g tins of chickpeas,
   drained and rinsed
1 x 400g tin of cherry
   tomatoes
1 x 400g tin of chopped
   tomatoes
200ml chicken stock
3 tbsp finely chopped
   parsley
200g spinach
2 tbsp sherry vinegar
Salt and pepper
Crusty bread, to serve

When at home, I love to cook big, bold, hearty dishes, like this rustic Spanish-style stew, which is perfect for a winter's day and can be left simmering away on the hob. If you fancy it, swap the chorizo for morcilla, the Spanish equivalent of black pudding.

1 Heat the olive oil in a large pot (with a lid) over a medium heat and gently fry the onion for 3–4 minutes until softened, then add the red and yellow peppers and cook for a further 5 minutes until softened. Do not let them brown.

2 Add the garlic and bay leaves and cook for a further minute, stirring frequently, then add the chorizo and cook for another 5 minutes, continuing to stir so the garlic doesn't burn or catch on the bottom of the pan. After 5 minutes, add the cayenne pepper and paprika, stir so everything is mixed well, and cook for 2 minutes. Add the chickpeas and cook for 3 minutes then add both the tinned cherry tomatoes and chopped tomatoes and cook for 2 minutes.

3 Finally, pour in the chicken stock, turn up the heat and bring to the boil. Reduce the heat by half and cook with the lid on for 45 minutes, stirring every so often to make sure nothing catches on the bottom of the pan.

4 After 45 minutes remove the lid from the pan and cook for a further 45 minutes without the lid, so the stew thickens. Stir regularly so it doesn't stick or burn.

5 After this time add the parsley and cook for 2 minutes. Add the spinach, put the lid on and cook for 2–3 minutes until wilted, then give it a good stir so it is all well mixed.

6 Season with salt and pepper. Mix in the sherry vinegar – you may want to add a little more to taste, but do taste it first. Remove the bay leaves and discard.

7 Drizzle with a little olive oil and serve with crusty bread.

PULLED PORK WITH→ APPLE & FENNEL SLAW

SERVES 6–8

FOR THE PORK

2–2.5kg pork shoulder
(off the bone)
1 tbsp sweet smoked
    paprika
1 tbsp ground cumin
1 tbsp coriander seeds
1 tsp cayenne pepper
2 star anise, broken up
1 tsp garlic powder
1 tbsp oregano
2 bay leaves, torn up
1 tbsp Maldon sea salt
¼ tsp black pepper
2 tbsp brown sugar
2 tbsp Worcestershire
    sauce
2 tbsp honey
500ml cider

FOR THE SLAW

1 large fennel bulb, outer
    layers removed, finely
    sliced (ideally with a
    mandolin)
¼ red cabbage, finely sliced
    (ideally with a mandolin)
½ red onion, finely sliced
1 red apple, cored and
    grated
1 carrot, grated
2 tbsp mayonnaise
Juice of ½ lemon
Salt and pepper

This recipe was written for two of my best mates, Elisha and Candy. I've never known anyone so addicted to pork as these girls. It's a great dish for when you have a lot of mates over, as the pork cooks slowly and fills the kitchen with amazing smells that will have you drooling long before it comes out of the oven. The apple and fennel slaw gives a fresh crunch that works really well alongside. The meat starts cooking hours in advance and the slaw can be made at the last minute, leaving you plenty of time for entertaining in between.

1. Place the pork shoulder into a large roasting tray.

2. Using a pestle and mortar, lightly crush together all the herbs and spices, along with the salt and pepper. Add the sugar, Worcestershire sauce, honey and 2 tablespoons of water and grind into a paste/sauce. Massage this paste into the pork. Cover with cling film and put in the fridge to marinate for 4 hours.

3. After marinating, remove the pork from the fridge 45 minutes before you wish to cook it, to allow it to warm up to room temperature. Take off the cling film.

4. Preheat the oven to 170°C/150°C fan/gas mark 3. Once the meat is at room temperature, add the cider to the roasting tray, cover with foil and cook in the oven for 6 hours. You want to check the liquid levels every 45–60 minutes and top up with water if needed.

5. In the final 30 minutes of the cooking time, prepare the slaw. In a large serving bowl, place the fennel, cabbage, onion and grated apple and carrot, add the mayonnaise and lemon juice, and season with salt and pepper to taste. Mix well.

6. After 6 hours, remove the pork from the oven and allow it to rest for 20 minutes.

FOR THE BARBECUE SAUCE

3 garlic cloves, peeled and grated
4cm piece of ginger, peeled and grated
150ml ketchup
150ml honey
150ml apple juice
3 tbsp Worcestershire sauce
2 tbsp smoked paprika
4 star anise
2 bay leaves
4 tbsp Dijon mustard

TO SERVE

6–8 soft white bread rolls

7 Meanwhile, make the barbecue sauce. Bring all the ingredients to the boil in a saucepan. Reduce to the lowest heat and simmer for 10 minutes until thickened. Whisk constantly so it doesn't catch on the bottom of the pan. Strain through a fine sieve to remove any bits.

8 When you are ready to serve, cut the fat off the pork and discard it along with the cooking liquid. Flake the meat, using forks or your fingers, so it's all nicely shredded.

9 Add a generous spoonful of the slaw to each bread roll, top with pork and finish with a spoonful of the barbecue sauce.

BRAISED BEEF CHEEKS WITH CELERIAC PURÉE & PARSNIP CRISPS

Beef cheeks are so, so tasty, and just melt in the mouth when cooked at a low heat for a long time. You probably won't find them in the supermarket but your local butcher is bound to have some. The celeriac purée may sound a bit posh, but it's easy to make and is a perfect match for the rich, mouth-watering cheeks. This is certainly a dish to impress.

SERVES 4

FOR THE BEEF CHEEKS

1kg beef cheeks (approx. 2 cheeks), trimmed of excess sinew and fat and the total portioned into 4 (ask your butcher to do this for you)

2 celery sticks, cut into 2cm chunks

1 medium onion, roughly sliced

2 carrots, peeled and cut into 1cm slices

1 tsp juniper berries

2 star anise

2 bay leaves

6 sprigs of thyme

1 tsp black peppercorns

375ml red wine (Cabernet Sauvignon)

500ml beef stock

1 tbsp Worcestershire sauce

1 tbsp tomato purée

1 tbsp sherry vinegar

Olive oil

Salt and pepper

1. Preheat the oven to 160°C/140°C fan/gas mark 3. Season the beef cheeks with salt and pepper.

2. Heat a large frying pan with a little olive oil over a high heat and brown the beef cheeks for 2–3 minutes on each side. You may need to do this in two batches. Once browned, put the cheeks into a casserole dish.

3. If there is lots of oil left in the frying pan, drain some off and then, in the same pan, soften the celery, onion and carrot over a low–medium heat for 5 minutes.

4. While they are softening, toast the juniper berries and star anise in a dry frying pan on a low heat for 2 minutes, and set them aside for a moment.

5. When the vegetables are softened, add the toasted juniper berries and star anise to the pan, along with the bay leaves, thyme and peppercorns. Stir well. Pour in the red wine and boil over a high heat until the mixture has reduced by a third.

6. Add in the beef stock, Worcestershire sauce, tomato purée and sherry vinegar and cook for 5 minutes until the sauce has thickened up. Check the seasoning and add salt if needed. Be careful, as the stock may already be salty and you don't want to over-season.

CONTINUES →

CONTINUED

FOR THE PARSNIP CRISPS
1 large parsnip
Fine salt
Vegetable oil, for frying

FOR THE CELERIAC PURÉE
1 large celeriac (400g), peeled
    and cut into 2cm chunks
250ml whole milk
250ml double cream
Salt and pepper

EQUIPMENT
Deep-fat fryer (or a deep
    saucepan and
    oil thermometer)

7. Pour the sauce into the casserole dish, put the lid on and cook for 3½–4 hours until the beef is tender and falling apart. Every hour, turn the cheeks and baste them, checking the liquid levels and adding water if needed.

8. While the beef is cooking, make the parsnip crisps and celeriac purée. Begin with the crisps. Preheat a deep-fat fryer to 180°C (or use a deep, heavy-based saucepan with an oil thermometer to regulate the temperature). Peel the parsnip, then top and tail it. Using a vegetable peeler, peel off thin slices of the parsnip to make shavings.

9. In batches, fry the parsnip shavings for 1–2 minutes, until golden, then drain them on kitchen paper and season with fine salt. Set the crisps aside until you're ready to serve.

10. Now, make the celeriac purée. Put the chunks of celeriac into a saucepan with the milk and cream. The celeriac should be submerged in liquid so top it up with water if necessary. Season with a good pinch of salt and simmer on a medium heat for 25–30 minutes until tender.

11. Using a slotted spoon, transfer the celeriac to a food processor. Add a few tablespoons of the cooking liquid, then blitz for 3–4 minutes, until you have a puré. You will not need to pass it through a sieve if you blend it for long enough: let the food processor do the work. You may need to add a little more of the cooking liquid if the purée is too thick. Season with pepper and taste to check whether more salt is needed. Keep warm until you are ready to serve.

12. When the beef is tender, remove it from the oven. If the sauce has not thickened up, strain it into a saucepan and heat on the hob for a further 5 minutes until thick and glossy.

13. To serve, remove the cheeks and strain the sauce into a jug, discarding the herbs and vegetables. Place portions of the celeriac purée on plates and a beef cheek portion alongside, then spoon some of the sauce over the meat. Top it off with the parsnip crisps.

BAKING IS SOMETHING I ASSOCIATE WITH GOOD HOME COOKING.

There's nothing quite as satisfying as creating the perfect cake or pie, and the smells that waft out of the kitchen never fail to put a smile on my face. Baking can help you switch off and unwind from everyday life; it can bring back childhood memories, and gather friends and families around the table.

I think baking is a skill that should be passed down the family from parent to child, or grandparent to grandchild, which is exactly what my nan did for me and my younger sister Carly. My earliest cooking memories are from my nan's kitchen when I was around 5 or 6 years old. We used to spend most weekends at her and my granddad's house, with Nan cooking mountains of food and us helping as much as we could, or usually just getting under her feet. We would run riot, nicking the chicken skin off our granddad's dinner and throwing tomato stalks in our Aunty Linda's bed and telling her there were spiders in her sheets! But Nan would spoil us rotten nonetheless. Looking back, I can see she was one of my biggest influences, and spending weekends in her kitchen is what helped get me into cooking.

Sundays were a day of feasting, and I remember everyone's happy faces as we all sat together as a family, enjoying Nan's creations. To this day I don't understand how we weren't the size of Violet Beauregarde when she blew up like a balloon in *Charlie and the Chocolate Factory*. We'd start with a full-on roast dinner and pud, and just a few hours later Nan would be back in the kitchen preparing a huge afternoon tea. She used to bake the most amazing corned beef hash pie, an old northern favourite (she was from Sunderland) that everyone always fought over. Sadly she took the recipe to her grave, but I've tried my best to recreate it from memory, and hopefully I've done it some justice (see page 105).

As a family, we have quite a sweet tooth, particularly my sister and mum (in fact I'm surprised they both still have a healthy set of gnashers!), so desserts are always an essential part of a family get-together. Some of our favourites are in this chapter and when I was writing the recipes for this book, naturally my mum and my sister were chief tasters, and even my dad gave a big thumbs-up to the apple and frangipane tart I made for his birthday celebrations.

SUN-DRIED TOMATO & BASIL twizzlers

MAKES 15–18

1 x 375g sheet of ready-
   rolled puff pastry
Plain flour, for dusting
50g Parmesan cheese,
   finely grated
Leaves from 2 basil sprigs,
   finely sliced
60g large sun-dried
   tomatoes, chopped
1 egg, beaten, for glazing
Maldon sea salt

These twizzlers make a nice change from ordinary cheese twists. Have fun inventing your own flavour combinations – you can also make sweet ones, such as cinnamon and raisin, chocolate and hazelnut, or twizzlers sprinkled with vanilla sugar.

1. Preheat the oven to 220°C/200°C fan/gas mark 7 and line a baking sheet with parchment paper.

2. Unroll the puff pastry onto a floured work surface and sprinkle it with two-thirds of the Parmesan, all the basil and all the sun-dried tomatoes.

3. Fold the sheet of pastry in half widthways, then, using a rolling pin, roll it back out to a rectangle 5mm thick. Chill in the fridge for 10 minutes to firm up.

4. Once firmed up, take it out of the fridge and cut it lengthways into 2cm-wide strips. You should get 15–18 strips. Twist each strip from end to end and place on the lined baking sheet.

5. Brush the strips with beaten egg, then sprinkle over the remaining cheese and a pinch of Maldon salt. Bake in the oven for 12 minutes, until golden and puffed up.

6. Remove the twizzlers from the oven and allow to cool on the baking tray. Serve straightaway once cool, or you can store in an airtight container for up to 2 days.

VARIATION

To make Gruyère Cheese and Thyme Twizzlers, follow the recipe above, omitting the sun-dried tomatoes and using 125g Gruyère cheese instead of Parmesan, and the leaves from 6 sprigs of thyme instead of basil. Lay out the pastry in the same way, sprinkling with two-thirds of the cheese and all the thyme, then continue with the method as above.

CRAB & SWEETCORN TARTLETS

SERVES 4

FOR THE TARTLETS
Plain flour, for dusting
375g ready-made shortcrust
   pastry
1 egg beaten with 1 tsp
   water (for an egg wash),
   plus 1 whole egg
100g white crabmeat
50g brown crabmeat
1 tbsp chopped coriander
1 red chilli, deseeded and
   finely chopped
40g cooked sweetcorn
100ml double cream
Salt and pepper

TO SERVE
100ml crème fraîche
Handful of rocket leaves
Juice of ½ lemon
2 tbsp olive oil

EQUIPMENT
4 x 10cm round, fluted,
   loose-bottomed tart tins

Crab and sweetcorn go beautifully together and these little tarts are great for a dinner party starter as they look and taste fantastic. It's best to buy your crabmeat fresh from a fishmonger, as you'll get much better quality and value for money than from a supermarket. Remember to check through the picked meat for any sharp bits of shell that may have been missed.

1 Preheat the oven to 180°C/160°C fan/gas mark 4.

2 Dust a work surface with flour. Divide the pastry into four equal pieces and roll each one out into a rough circle about 16cm in diameter. Lift each piece into a tin and gently press it into the bottom and up the sides, but don't trim off the edges yet.

3 Prick the pastry bases all over with a fork, place a circle of parchment paper on top of each base, fill the cases with an even layer of baking beans and place in the oven to bake for 15 minutes.

4 Take the cases out of the oven, remove the beans and paper and return to the oven for another 5 minutes.

5 Brush the base and sides of each tarlet case with the egg wash and return to the oven for a further 3 minutes.

6 While the cases are baking, make the filling. In a large bowl mix the crabmeats, coriander, chilli and sweetcorn, and season with a little salt and pepper. Once the pastry cases have been baked with the egg wash, divide the crab mixture evenly between them.

7 In a measuring jug, whisk together the whole egg and double cream, and season with salt and pepper. Pour about a quarter of the egg/cream liquid into each case and bake in the oven for a further 20–25 minutes until the filling has set.

8 Remove from the oven and allow to cool slightly, then neatly trim the pastry edges and remove the tartlets from their tins.

9 Serve warm or cold with a dollop of crème fraîche and rocket leaves dressed with the lemon juice and olive oil.

Nan's FAMOUS CORNED BEEF HASH PIE

My nan was a brilliant cook. In fact, my love of food first started in her kitchen, where she would spend time with me and my sister, teaching us how to make cakes and other treats. Most of the ingredients would end up down our fronts, and we always fought over who got to lick the bowl at the end (typical kids!), but nevertheless we had great fun. Another cooking delight that everyone in our family used to fight over was her amazing corned beef hash pie. Sadly, I don't know her exact recipe, but this is my take on it, inspired by childhood memories.

1. Preheat the oven to 180°C/160°C fan/gas mark 4.

2. Heat the olive oil in a frying pan over a medium heat, add the onion and the whole sprig of rosemary and cook for 2–3 minutes until the onion is gently softened.

3. Add the corned beef and Worcestershire sauce and cook for 5 minutes on a low–medium heat. Remove from the heat and scrape the mixture into a bowl, discarding the rosemary sprig. Allow to cool to room temperature.

4. When cooled, mix the corned beef with the mashed potatoes in a large bowl until well combined. Season with salt and pepper.

5. Set aside one-third of the pastry for the pie lid. On a floured work surface, roll out the remaining two-thirds into a 30cm circle the thickness of a pound coin. Place the pie dish upside down in the centre and cut around it, allowing a 1cm excess all the way around. Ease the pastry into the pie dish, pressing it firmly into the sides. Roll out the pastry reserved for the lid into a 25cm circle.

6. Fill the lined pie dish with the cooled beef and potato mixture, remembering to put the pie bird/funnel in the centre if you're using one. Brush the edges of the pastry with beaten egg and place the lid on top. Using a small, sharp knife held at a 45-degree angle, cut around the edge of the pie to remove any excess pastry. Crimp the edges with your fingers or a fork, and brush all over the top with beaten egg. If not using a pie funnel, cut two slits in the centre of the lid to allow steam to escape. Using the leftover bits of pastry, cut out four leaves, brush with beaten egg and place in the middle of the lid, pointing outwards.

7. Bake the pie in the oven for 35–45 minutes, checking after 35 minutes to see if the top is golden and crisp. If not, leave it in for the remaining 5–10 minutes.

8. When cooked, allow to cool for 15–20 minutes before serving. The pie can be eaten warm or cold.

SERVES 6

1 tbsp olive oil
1 medium onion, finely diced
1 rosemary sprig
340g tinned corned beef, chopped into 2cm chunks
1 tbsp Worcestershire sauce
500g mashed potato (roughly 3 medium potatoes), mashed with 30g butter and cooled to room temperature
1 x 500g block of ready-made shortcrust pastry
Plain flour, for dusting
1 egg, beaten, for glazing
Salt and pepper

EQUIPMENT
22cm round pie dish
Pie bird or funnel (optional)

PEA & HAM QUICHE

On Sundays when I was growing up, my nan always used to make us afternoon tea. She would whip up all sorts of goodies, like sausage rolls, her special corned beef hash pie (see page 105) and quiche, which I love. Pea and ham is such a British combination and a match made in heaven. So this quiche was certainly a winner with my family on those Sunday afternoons.

SERVES 6

20g unsalted butter, plus extra for greasing
Plain flour, for dusting
1 x 500g block of ready-made shortcrust pastry
1 egg, beaten with 1 tsp water (for an egg wash), plus 3 medium eggs
½ medium onion, finely diced
250ml chicken stock
150g fresh peas
200g cooked ham hock, chopped into 1cm dice
1 tbsp sliced fresh mint
200ml double cream
Salt and pepper

EQUIPMENT

23cm round, fluted, loose-bottomed flan tin or quiche dish, 2.5cm deep

1. Grease the quiche tin or dish with butter. On a floured work surface, roll out the pastry to the thickness of a pound coin. Cut out a circle big enough to fill the quiche tin/dish and hang over the sides, about 30–32cm in diameter. Press it into the base of the tin and up the sides, but don't trim off the edges yet. Chill in the fridge for 20 minutes to firm up.

2. Meanwhile, preheat the oven to 190°C/170°C fan/gas mark 5. Prick the chilled pastry base all over with a fork, place a circle of parchment paper on top of the base, fill the case with an even layer of baking beans and place in the oven to bake for 20 minutes.

3. Take it out of the oven, remove the beans and paper and return to the oven for another 5 minutes. Remove from the oven and reduce the oven temperature to 170°C/150°C fan/gas mark 3.

4. Gently brush the base and sides of the pastry with the egg wash and return to the oven for a further 3 minutes.

5. While the pastry is baking, make the filling. Melt the butter in a frying pan on a gentle heat and cook the onion for about 3 minutes until softened but not brown. Remove from the heat and allow to cool.

6. Bring the chicken stock to the boil in a pan, add the peas and cook for 1–2 minutes until softened, then drain and cool.

7. In a bowl, mix the softened onions, drained peas, ham and mint, ready to fill the quiche. In another bowl, whisk the three eggs with the cream and season well with salt and pepper.

8. Once the pastry case has been blind-baked, fill with the pea/ham mixture and pour over the cream/egg mixture.

9. Bake in the oven for 35–40 minutes until the filling has set. Remove from the oven and allow to cool slightly, then neatly trim the edges of the pastry and remove the quiche from the tin.

BUTTERNUT SQUASH & MASCARPONE TART

SERVES 6–8

1 medium butternut
squash, peeled and
chopped into 1–2cm
chunks (chopped
weight 650g)
Leaves from 1 rosemary
sprig
1 tbsp olive oil, plus extra
for drizzling
25g butter
1½ large red onions, sliced
1 tbsp caster sugar
4–5 tbsp balsamic vinegar
1 x 375g sheet of ready-
rolled puff pastry
2 tbsp pine nuts
4–5 tbsp mascarpone
cheese
1 red chilli, finely sliced,
or ½ tsp dried chilli
flakes (optional)
1 egg, beaten, for glazing
Handful of rocket leaves,
to garnish (optional)
Salt and pepper

This tart is so fast and simple to make but definitely
delivers on taste. Ready-rolled puff pastry makes life
really easy here. You can swap the mascarpone for
feta if you prefer its tangy flavour.

1 Preheat the oven to 220°C/200°C fan/gas mark 7.

2 Place the butternut squash in a baking tray and sprinkle with
the rosemary leaves. Drizzle with a good glug of olive oil and
season with salt. Bake in the oven for 20–25 minutes until the
butternut squash is tender.

3 Meanwhile, in a frying pan set on a low heat, warm the
tablespoon of olive oil and melt the butter. Add the onions,
sugar and 4 tablespoons of balsamic vinegar, and season well
with salt and pepper. Cook gently for 20–25 minutes until the
onions are softened and caramelised. Taste the onions while
cooking, as you may need to add the extra spoonful of vinegar.

4 Just before the butternut squash and onions are ready, unroll
the pastry onto a large baking sheet and score a border around
the pastry about 1.5cm from the edge, like a picture frame. Using
a fork, prick all over the pastry inside the 'frame'.

5 When the squash and onions are ready, remove the onions from
the pan using a slotted spoon to ensure that any excess oil is left
behind. Spread the onions evenly over the centre of the pastry
(staying within the border), scatter with the squash, sprinkle on
the pine nuts and dollop the mascarpone on top. Season with a
little more salt and a good grinding of pepper. Sprinkle with the
chopped red chilli or chilli flakes, if using. Brush the border with
beaten egg, so you get a nice shine on the pastry.

6 Bake in the oven for 25–30 minutes until golden brown. Garnish
with rocket leaves, if using.

tomato, MOZZARELLA & CARAMELISED ONION TART

This is a classic combination of flavours, presented in a beautiful way. I tend to use ready-rolled pastry for recipes like this as it's fast and easy, and you end up with a stunning tart for not much work. If you fancy slightly stronger flavours, keep the tomatoes and caramelised onions, but omit the mozzarella, replace the basil with thyme, and finish with Gruyère cheese.

SERVES 6–8

1 tbsp olive oil, plus extra for drizzling

25g butter

3 red onions, sliced

5 tbsp balsamic vinegar, plus a bit extra to taste

1 tbsp sugar, plus an extra pinch for the tomatoes

1 x 375g sheet of ready-rolled puff pastry

1 egg, beaten, for glazing

200g baby plum tomatoes, halved

12 basil leaves, finely sliced

2 balls of mozzarella, finely sliced

Salt and pepper

1 Heat the oil and butter in a frying pan set on a low heat. Add the onions, vinegar and sugar and season well with salt and pepper. Cook gently for 20–25 minutes until softened and caramelised. Taste the onions while cooking, as you may need to add an extra spoonful or two of vinegar. Towards the end, preheat the oven to 220°C/200°C fan/gas mark 7.

2 Unroll the pastry onto a large baking sheet and score a border around the pastry about 1.5cm from the edge, like a picture frame. Using a fork, prick all over the pastry inside the 'frame'.

3 Spread the caramelised onions over the centre of the pastry (within the border) and brush the border with beaten egg so you get a nice shine on the pastry. Bake in the oven for 20 minutes.

4 Meanwhile, mix the tomatoes and basil leaves in a mixing bowl and season with salt and a little pinch of sugar.

5 After 20 minutes, remove the tart from the oven, scatter over the tomatoes and basil, and arrange the mozzarella on top. Drizzle with a little olive oil and season with pepper and a little salt, then continue to cook the tart for 5 minutes so the cheese melts slightly.

SPELT SCONES

Afternoon tea is one of the things us Brits are famous for and do so well. My mum loves afternoon tea so a few times a year my sister and I like to treat her, taking her to London to a hotel or café to indulge in cakes, scones and elegant finger sandwiches. Scones was one of the first things I made in school and it is one of the things my mum loves the most. So when I'm in baking mode I like to make a big batch of scones as a treat for her. I've replaced normal flour with spelt flour in this recipe as spelt is suitable for people with a wheat intolerance. I like to serve my scones warm and with a good dollop of my Zingtastic Lemon & Lime Curd (see page 216).

MAKES 16

500g spelt flour, plus extra
    for dusting
4 tsp baking powder
Pinch of salt
90g unsalted butter,
    chilled and cubed
75g caster sugar
2 eggs, beaten plus 1 egg
beaten with 1 tbsp
    water (for an egg wash)
200ml whole milk
Zingtastic Lemon & Lime
    Curd, to serve (see page
    216)

1 Preheat the oven to 220°C/200°C fan/gas mark 7.

2 Sift the flour, baking powder and salt into a mixing bowl. Add the butter and rub it into the flour with the tips of your fingers until the mixture resembles breadcrumbs.

3 Add the sugar and eggs and mix in using a wooden spoon. Pour in a third of the milk and mix gently, then mix in the remaining milk a little bit at a time. You want to bring the ingredients together into a rough dough.

4 Turn out onto a floured work surface and knead the dough until it becomes smooth. Be careful not to overwork or it will become too stiff.

5 Dust a rolling pin with flour and roll out the dough to a thickness of 2.5cm. Using a 5cm scone/cookie cutter, cut out the scones until all the dough has been used up, dipping the cutter into some flour before each one, to help stop it sticking.

6 Brush the scones all over with the egg wash, using a pastry brush. Place them on a lightly greased baking tray and bake in the oven for 15 minutes, until risen and golden brown.

7 Remove from the oven and leave to cool on a wire rack. To serve, cut in half and spread with a little butter and some of my Zingtastic Lemon & Lime Curd.

CLEMENTINE MADELEINES WITH CLEMENTINE POSSET

Clementines always remind me of Christmas, my favourite time of year. So I've gone all out and used them in two ways here: a smooth, creamy posset (a medieval drink that's evolved into a set, thickened cream dessert), and lovely soft madeleine cakes. Obviously, you can make these all year round, not just for Christmas – swap the clementines with lemons or even limes to suit the season. For the prettiest madeleines, try to find a traditional tin with decorative holes.

SERVES 6 (MAKES 24 MADELEINES)

FOR THE MADELEINES
3 eggs
125g caster sugar
125g plain flour
Pinch of salt
½ tsp baking powder
Finely grated zest of
 ½ clementine
1 tsp vanilla paste
100g butter, melted, plus
 extra for greasing
Icing sugar, for dusting

FOR THE CLEMENTINE POSSETS
125g caster sugar
Juice of 4 clementines
Finely grated zest of
 1 clementine, plus strips
 of zest (use a zester) to
 decorate (optional)
500ml double cream

EQUIPMENT
1 x 12-hole madeleine tray
6 x 100ml ramekins or jars

1 You need to begin this recipe the day before you want to serve it. Start by making the madeleine batter. Place the eggs and sugar in a mixing bowl and beat with an electric whisk for 5 minutes until they become pale, fluffy and thick.

2 In another mixing bowl, combine the flour, salt and baking powder. Add the clementine zest and vanilla paste to the egg mixture, then sift in half the flour mixture and fold it in with a spatula or metal spoon. Repeat with the other half of the flour. Try not to over-fold, or the batter will deflate.

3 Fold in half the melted butter, followed by the other half. Pour the mixture into an airtight container and leave to rest in the fridge overnight.

4 The clementine posset also needs to be made a day ahead. Bring the sugar, clementine juice and zest to the boil in a saucepan. Remove from the heat as soon as it reaches boiling point (the sugar will have dissolved).

5 In a separate pan, bring the double cream to boiling point, then remove from the heat. Whisk in the clementine mixture, pour it into the ramekins or jars and allow to cool. Once cooled, place in the fridge to set completely overnight.

6 The next day, preheat the oven to 190°C/170°C fan/gas mark 5. Remove the madeleine batter from the fridge about 30 minutes before you want to bake them (you'll need to bake in two batches).

7 Grease the madeleine tin with melted butter using a pastry brush, then spoon about a tablespoon of batter into each hole (remember that you are only using half the batter for the first batch). When all the holes are filled, tap the tin on the work surface to even out the batter and expel any air.

8 Bake in the oven for 15–20 minutes until the cakes are golden and spring back when pressed. When ready, remove from the oven and allow to cool slightly on a wire rack. Repeat with the second batch.

9 Dust the madeleines with icing sugar and serve two warm madeleines with each posset. Decorate the possets with a few strips of clementine zest. The remaining madeleines will keep for up to 2 days in an airtight container.

RHUBARB MESS

SERVES 4

FOR THE MERINGUES
3 large egg whites
150g caster sugar
½ tsp white wine vinegar

FOR THE RHUBARB COMPOTE
600g fresh rhubarb, ends removed and cut into 2cm pieces
60g golden caster sugar
Grated zest of ½ orange
1 star anise

FOR THE VANILLA CREAM
400ml double cream
4 tbsp icing sugar
1 tbsp vanilla paste

TO SERVE
2 ginger biscuits, blitzed to fine crumbs

I had my parents over for dinner one Sunday and wanted to make them a simple dessert. As it wasn't summer, the idea of Eton mess went out the window, but it was rhubarb season, so I invented rhubarb mess instead! My mum loves rhubarb, so this has become one of her favourite puds.

1 Preheat the oven to 160°C/140°C fan/gas mark 3 and line a baking sheet with parchment paper.

2 Whisk the egg whites to stiff peaks with an electric mixer or whisk. Add the sugar, a tablespoon at a time, whisking well between each addition. By the end, the mixture will be glossy and stiff – and you should be able to hold the bowl upside down (over your head if you dare!) and it stays put.

3 Fold in the vinegar with a spatula, then spoon the meringue mixture onto the baking tray so that it is 2–3cm thick.

4 Put the meringue in the oven, immediately reducing the temperature to 150°C/130°C fan/gas mark 2, and bake for 45 minutes or until the outside of the meringue is set; the inside will still be chewy. Leave to cool on the baking tray. Once cooled, break into pieces.

5 While the meringue is cooking, make the rhubarb compote. Place all the compote ingredients into a large saucepan and cook on a medium heat for 20–25 minutes until the rhubarb breaks down. Keep an eye on it, and if it looks dry add a tablespoon of water. When cooked, remove the star anise and drain off any excess liquid, then allow to cool to room temperature before serving.

6 To make the vanilla cream, use a whisk or electric mixer to beat the ingredients together until they form stiff peaks, then set aside until ready to serve.

7 When you are ready to serve, place the broken meringue pieces into a large bowl, then gently fold through the vanilla cream. Also fold in the rhubarb compote, but don't combine too well as you want a rippled mixture of pink and white, not a uniform pink. Spoon into serving bowls and top with the ginger crumbs.

APRICOT & ALMOND CLAFOUTIS

SERVES 6–8

FOR THE CLAFOUTIS
3 eggs, plus 1 extra egg
   yolk
150g caster sugar, plus
   2 tbsp extra
100g plain flour
50g ground almonds
1 tbsp vanilla paste
Grated zest of ½ orange
25g unsalted butter,
   melted, plus extra for
   greasing
125ml whole milk
125ml double cream
6 apricots (approx. 450g
   total), halved and
   stoned
50g flaked toasted
   almonds, to serve
   (optional)

FOR THE VANILLA CREAM
300ml double cream
1 tbsp vanilla paste
3 tbsp icing sugar

EQUIPMENT
1.2-litre round baking dish,
   5cm deep

A clafoutis is a French, batter-based dessert that's typically made with cherries, but I've given the recipe a twist and instead used soft apricots and ground almonds, which go really well with the custardy batter. When apricots aren't in season, you can use other soft fruits like plums, cherries or blueberries instead.

1 Preheat the oven to 180°C/160°C fan/gas mark 4.

2 Place the whole eggs, extra yolk and caster sugar in a mixing bowl, and whisk with an electric mixer or whisk for 4–5 minutes until pale and fluffy.

3 Sift in the flour, then fold it in with a spatula or metal spoon, followed by the ground almonds. Gently fold in the vanilla paste, orange zest and melted butter. Finally fold in the milk and cream so that everything is incorporated.

4 Grease the baking dish with butter, then coat it with the 2 tablespoons of sugar, spinning the dish so it is evenly coated.

5 Pour in the batter mixture, then arrange the apricots in the batter, peeking out the top. Bake in the oven for 45 minutes to 1 hour, until set, testing by inserting a knife or skewer: if it comes out clean, the clafoutis is ready.

6 Meanwhile, to prepare the vanilla cream, whisk all the ingredients until they form medium-firm peaks. Set aside until ready to serve.

7 Remove the clafoutis from the oven and allow to cool for a few minutes, then scatter with the flaked almonds and serve in bowls with a dollop of the vanilla cream.

ORANGE OLIVE OIL CAKE

SERVES 6–8

FOR THE CAKE
200g spelt flour
Pinch of salt
2 tsp baking powder
Grated zest of 1½ oranges
200g caster sugar
3 eggs
60ml whole milk
175ml olive oil

FOR THE ORANGE CREAM
200ml double cream
2 tbsp icing sugar
Grated zest of ½ orange
1 tbsp Cointreau (optional)

EQUIPMENT
20cm round, springform
    cake tin

This cake reminds me a bit of a (very big!) madeleine, because of its citrus tang. The olive oil helps to keep it perfectly moist. You can use orange olive oil if you can source it, to enhance the orange flavour even more.

1 Preheat the oven to 180°C/160°C fan/gas mark 4. Grease the base of the cake tin and line with parchment paper.

2 Mix the flour, salt and baking powder in a mixing bowl until well combined.

3 In another bowl, combine the orange zest and sugar. Add the eggs and beat with an electric whisk until light and fluffy. Whisk in the milk, then the olive oil.

4 Using a spatula or metal spoon, gradually fold the flour mixture into the egg mixture until incorporated. Pour the mixture into the greased and lined cake tin.

5 Bake the cake in the oven for 35–40 minutes. To test if it is cooked, insert a skewer through the middle and, if it comes out clean, it's ready. If not, return to the oven for a few minutes before testing again.

6 Leave to cool on a wire rack for 10 minutes and then remove from the tin.

7 Meanwhile, make the orange cream. Whisk the double cream and icing sugar until they form stiff peaks, then fold in the orange zest and Cointreau.

8 You can serve the cake warm or cold, with a dollop of the orange cream. Store the cake in an airtight container for up to 3 days.

SALTED CARAMEL BROWNIES

This is a great twist on regular brownies, with hidden pieces of salted caramel that just melt in your mouth. Once you start eating, you probably won't be able to stop until the entire tray has gone... you have been warned!

1. Start with the salted caramel. This recipe makes double the required quantity, but it's tricky to make in smaller quantities as it's more likely to burn. Use the extra for another recipe or see the tip, opposite.

2. In a saucepan over a medium heat, melt the butter, sugar and 1 tablespoon of water, swirling the pan every so often (but making sure you do not stir). You want it to become golden brown, but keep a close eye on it as caramel can easily burn. When it is bubbling and golden brown, the smell will change to a honey-like scent. At this point, remove from the heat and whisk in the salt and cream. Be very careful, as it will be extremely hot. Leave to cool for 5 minutes.

3. Line a baking dish or bowl with cling film, pour in the salted caramel and leave on the side to set for around 30 minutes. When set, flip out onto a chopping board. Put half away for another day and chop the rest into rough chunks. Set aside, until ready to bake the brownies.

4. Preheat the oven to 180°C/160°C fan/gas mark 4 and line the tin with parchment paper.

5. Place a heatproof bowl over a saucepan of simmering water and melt the chocolate and butter in it. Do not let the bottom of the bowl touch the water. When melted, remove from the heat and leave the mixture to cool for about 5 minutes.

6. In a mixing bowl, whisk together the eggs and sugar until pale and fluffy. Whisk in the vanilla paste. Sift half the flour into the egg mixture, fold in with a spatula or metal spoon, then sift in the remaining flour, add the salt, and fold in.

7. Fold in the melted chocolate/butter and when mixed well, fold in the pecans and half the chopped salted caramel.

8. Pour the mixture into the lined tin. Add the remaining chopped caramel on top and bake for 35–40 minutes until the crust looks set, dry and pale brown, and cracks slightly if you press it gently. Don't be tempted to bake for longer as you want the brownies to stay gooey in the middle.

9. Remove from the oven and let the brownies stand for 5 minutes before cutting into pieces and removing from the tin.

MAKES 12

FOR THE BROWNIES
100g dark chocolate,
    min. 70% cocoa solids,
    broken into pieces
120g unsalted butter,
    chopped into small cubes
2 large eggs
200g caster sugar
1 tsp vanilla paste
100g plain flour
Pinch of salt
40g pecans, roughly
    chopped

FOR THE SALTED
CARAMEL
150g caster sugar
50g unsalted butter
1 tsp fine sea salt
3 tbsp double cream

EQUIPMENT
20cm square baking tin

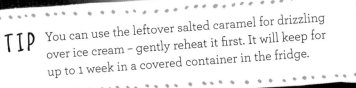

TIP You can use the leftover salted caramel for drizzling over ice cream – gently reheat it first. It will keep for up to 1 week in a covered container in the fridge.

APPLE FRANGIPANE TART

For his birthday, my dad requested an apple pie or tart, so I came up with this. It's simple to prepare but looks very impressive, with the apple slices layered in a beautiful spiral pattern on top of frangipane, which is a sweet almond-flavoured filling. The tart is best served straight from the oven. You can also make it with pears.

1 In a food processor, blitz the butter and sugar until pale and fluffy. Add the ground almonds, flour and egg, and pulse until the mixture comes together. This is the frangipane. (If you don't have a food processor, use an electric hand whisk.)

2 Using a spatula, remove the frangipane from the food processor and put it in a bowl. Cover with cling film and chill in the fridge for at least 30 minutes to firm up.

3 Lightly oil a large flat baking sheet and line with parchment paper. On a floured work surface, roll out the puff pastry to the thickness of a pound coin. Place a 25cm round dinner plate on top of the pastry and cut around it to get a circle. Remove the dinner plate and discard the excess pastry or save in the fridge for something else.

4 Put the pastry onto the lined baking sheet, then crimp up the edges of the pastry using your fingers and thumbs so it forms a 1cm edge/wall. Place in the fridge to firm up for 20 minutes. Preheat the oven to 200°C/180°C fan/gas mark 6. Using a mandolin or a sharp knife, slice the apples into 0.5cm slices (whole rings) and set aside.

5 When the pastry is firm and the frangipane is chilled, remove both from the fridge. Gently prick the base of the pastry all over with a fork but do not pierce all the way through. Spoon the frangipane into the centre of the tart and spread out evenly.

6 Starting from the outside, layer the apple rings in a clockwise direction, overlapping each ring so it just covers the hole in the previous one. Do this until you have an outer circle, then repeat with an inner circle and finally a small circle in the middle, until the whole tart is covered.

7 Sprinkle with the extra caster sugar and dot with the extra butter. Brush the pastry edges with the egg wash. Bake the tart in the oven for 35–45 minutes until crisp and golden.

8 Meanwhile, make the vanilla cream. In a mixing bowl, whisk all the ingredients together until they form medium-firm peaks.

9 Allow the cooked tart to cool for 5 minutes before dusting with icing sugar and serving with the vanilla cream.

SERVES 6–8

FOR THE TART
100g unsalted butter, cubed, plus 15g for glazing
100g caster sugar, plus 1 tbsp for glazing
100g ground almonds
1 tbsp plain flour, plus extra for dusting
1 egg, plus 1 egg beaten with 1 tsp water (for an egg wash)
320g ready-made puff pastry
4 Cox or Granny Smith apples, peeled and cored but kept whole
Icing sugar, for dusting

FOR THE VANILLA CREAM
300ml double cream
3 tbsp icing sugar
1 tbsp vanilla paste

5 EN

PAPILLOTE

WHEN I TOLD FRIENDS THAT I WANTED TO INCLUDE AN 'EN PAPILLOTE' section

in my book , there were many there were many confused faces. But when I explained that 'papillote' is just a posh French term for 'cooking in a bag/parcel', everyone laughed. I know from experience that things which sound alien or complicated can put you off cooking, especially if you're a beginner or don't have much confidence, but the truth is that most of those fancy cooking terms actually refer to very simple techniques. At one time or another, you have probably cooked 'en papillote' without even knowing it. Ever baked something wrapped up in foil? There you go!

This is a really great way of cooking, and you can serve the finished dish still in its parcel. The bag traps in all the moisture, flavours and aromas of your ingredients, so when you open it up at the dinner table, those amazing smells hit you straight away and you don't lose any of them between dishing up and tucking in (unlike when you roast, when the aromas escape into the air throughout the cooking process).

You can go savoury or sweet in this chapter, and I've included some fun recipes like Pimp my Corn, with four delicious popcorn flavours – perfect for a film night, and Gooey Chocolate Bananas, which is my Bonfire Night special. It's a wrap!

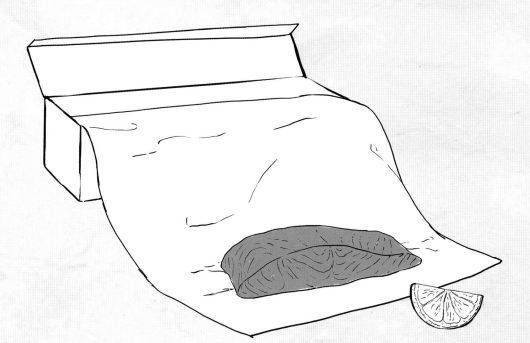

SALMON & COURGETTE EN PAPILLOTE

SERVES 4

300g topped/tailed
   courgettes (about 2
   medium ones)
4 tsp capers, rinsed
4 tsp lemon juice
12 basil leaves, finely sliced
4 x salmon fillets (approx.
   200g each)
2 whole lemons
Olive oil
Salt and pepper

This very simple salmon recipe can be made in just minutes. The courgettes, lemon, basil and capers work in harmony with the salmon, adding lots of contrasting flavours and an extra hit of freshness.

1 Preheat the oven to 200°C/180°C fan/gas mark 6.

2 Measure out four rectangles of parchment paper, 50cm x 25cm, then fold each in half into a square.

3 Using a vegetable peeler, slice the courgettes lengthways to make ribbons. Place into a bowl and add the capers, lemon juice and basil. Season with salt and pepper, and drizzle with olive oil.

4 Open up the folded parchment squares and divide the courgettes evenly between the four parcels, positioning them in the middle of the bottom square of paper.

5 Place a salmon fillet on top of the courgettes, season with salt and pepper and drizzle with a little olive oil.

6 Slice the lemons thinly and place two slices on top of each salmon fillet. Fold over the top half of the paper, then fold up the edges of the square to make a parcel around the salmon and courgettes.

7 Place the parcels on a baking tray and bake in the oven for 15 minutes.

8 Remove from the oven and serve still in the parcels.

CHICKEN CHERMOULA

SERVES 4

4 skinless chicken breasts
(approx. 150g each)

FOR THE CHERMOULA
1 tbsp pink peppercorns
1 tbsp coriander seeds
1 tbsp cumin seeds
½ tsp cayenne pepper
½ tsp ground cinnamon
1 tbsp smoked paprika
1 tsp Maldon sea salt
2 garlic cloves, crushed
3 tbsp fresh coriander,
   finely chopped, plus
   extra for serving
3 tbsp fresh parsley, finely
   chopped
Grated zest of 1 lemon
4 tbsp olive oil

TO SERVE
Rice or couscous
Chopped coriander
1 lemon, cut into 4 wedges

Chermoula is a herby marinade commonly used in North-African cooking. I only discovered it recently when I saw it on a menu, and there are many different variations, but this is my take on it. It works really well with chicken breast, and cooking 'en papillote' keeps the meat juicy and moist. You can also use it to marinate fish or steaks.

1. In a small, dry frying pan, gently toast the pink peppercorns, coriander and cumin seeds for 1–2 minutes, until they give off their aromas.

2. Once toasted, place the spices into a pestle and mortar and grind to a powder. Add the rest of the spices, the salt and garlic and grind further, until it starts to become a paste. Add the fresh herbs, lemon zest and olive oil and grind/muddle until everything is well combined.

3. Place the chicken breasts into food/freezer bags or a mixing bowl, cover with the marinade and mix well. Leave to marinate for at least 4 hours, preferably overnight.

4. Preheat the oven to 190°C/170°C fan/gas mark 5.

5. Measure out four rectangles of parchment paper, 50cm x 25cm, and then fold each in half into a square.

6. Open up the folded parchment and place a chicken breast in the middle of each bottom square. Fold over the top half of the paper, then fold up the edges to seal the squares into parcels, place them onto a baking tray and cook for 25–30 minutes. To check the chicken is cooked, stick a skewer or knife into the chicken breast: if the juices run clear then it's ready. If not, return to the oven for a few minutes before testing again.

7. Serve with rice or couscous, scattered with freshly chopped coriander, and a lemon wedge on the side.

ASIAN-*Style* MACKEREL IN A BAG

FOR THE BAG

4 heads of pak choi

100g beansprouts

6 spring onions, finely chopped

8 mackerel fillets (approx. 100g each)

2 spring onions, finely sliced

1 red chilli, deseeded and finely sliced

2 tbsp finely chopped coriander

2 tbsp sesame seeds

1 lime, cut into 4 wedges

FOR THE SAUCE

4 tbsp soy sauce

4 tbsp mirin or rice wine vinegar

4 tbsp sesame oil

4 tbsp honey

2 tsp chilli flakes

5cm piece of ginger, peeled and grated

2 garlic cloves, peeled and grated

I love mackerel and think it's a really underrated fish. It can have a pretty strong taste, so these bold Asian flavours work perfectly with it. This is great served with sticky rice or noodles.

1 Preheat the oven to 200°C/180°C fan/gas mark 6.

2 Measure out four rectangles of parchment paper, 50cm x 30cm, and then fold each in half into near-squares.

3 Open up the folded paper and divide the pak choi, beansprouts and chopped spring onions between the four parcels, placing them in the middle of the bottom squares of paper. Place two mackerel fillets on top of each pile of vegetables.

4 Fold over the top half of the paper and fold up two sides of each parcel to seal, leaving one side open.

5 In a small mixing bowl, whisk all the ingredients for the sauce until well combined, then spoon this evenly between the parcels. Seal the final edge of each parcel.

6 Place the parcels on a baking tray and bake in the oven for 12 minutes.

7 Remove the parcels from the oven and open them. Serve the fish and vegetables in bowls, pour over the cooking juices and scatter with the spring onions, chilli, coriander and sesame seeds (divided evenly). Serve with a lime wedge on the side.

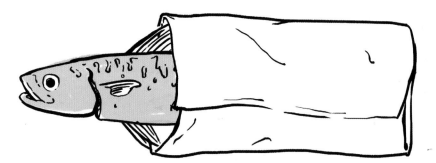

MUSTARDY PORK CHOP & LEEK PARCELS

SERVES 4

- 4 pork chops (approx. 225g each)
- 2 tbsp olive oil
- 20g butter
- 3 leeks, finely sliced
- 1 banana or Echalion shallot, finely sliced
- 75ml chicken stock
- 300ml crème fraîche
- 1 tbsp wholegrain mustard
- 1 tbsp finely chopped parsley
- 1 tbsp finely chopped tarragon
- Salt and pepper

Cooking pork can be a tricky business as it can dry out easily, but doing it in a parcel like this works well because it keeps the meat moist, as well as being simple and fuss-free. You can also make this recipe using chicken if you fancy a change, as the mustard and leek sauce is really versatile.

1 Preheat the oven to 200°C/180°C fan/gas mark 6.

2 Prepare the chops by making cuts in the fat/rind every 2cm. This will stop the chops from curling up and also help to render the fat and get it crispy. When all the chops are prepared, season both sides well with salt and pepper.

3 Heat a large frying pan with 1 tablespoon of olive oil and the butter over a medium heat. In two batches, sear the chops for 1–2 minutes on each side until brown, basting with the melted butter in the pan as they cook. When they are brown on both sides, set aside.

4 In another deep frying pan, heat the other tablespoon of olive oil on a medium heat and cook the leeks and shallots for 3–4 minutes until tender. Be careful not to brown them. Add the chicken stock and bring to the boil, then reduce the heat by half and add the crème fraîche and mustard. Cook for 3–4 minutes until it thickens a little.

5 Add the parsley and tarragon and cook for another 2 minutes, then remove from the heat and season with salt and pepper.

6 Measure out a piece of foil 80cm x 30cm, fold it in half and put it into a roasting tin. Open up the folded foil and pour half the leek mixture into the tray onto the bottom piece, lay the chops on top and cover with the remaining leek mixture.

7 Fold over the top half of the foil, scrunch up all the sides of the parcel to seal and put the roasting tin into the oven for 30 minutes.

8 When cooked, remove the roasting tray from the oven, open the parcel and serve straightaway, spooning the leek sauce generously over the top of the chops.

WILD MUSHROOMS WITH HERB BUTTER

SERVES 4

400g mixed wild
 mushrooms
4 tbsp finely chopped
 parsley
2 tbsp finely chopped
 tarragon
2 garlic cloves, crushed
50g butter
8 slices of sourdough bread
Olive oil, for drizzling
Salt and pepper

I absolutely love wild mushrooms. This recipe takes just minutes to prepare and the end result is so tasty. It makes a lovely brunch or you can serve it as a simple starter. Be adventurous and try out different types of mushrooms – exotic ones like shiitake and enoki work well. To add a touch of luxury, you can even finish with a splash of truffle oil.

1. Preheat the oven to 200°C/180°C fan/gas mark 6.

2. Make sure the mushrooms are clean and grit-free. Using a pastry brush, you can lightly brush any dirt or grit away.

3. Measure out a rectangle of parchment paper, 60cm x 30cm, then fold it in half into a square.

4. Open up the folded parchment and place the mushrooms in the middle of the bottom square of paper. Scatter with the parsley, tarragon and garlic, dot with the butter and season with salt and pepper. Fold over the top half of the paper, then fold up the edges of the square to seal the parcel and place it on a baking tray. Bake for 10-12 minutes until the mushrooms have softened. Be careful not to overcook them.

5. While the mushrooms are cooking, heat a griddle pan on a medium–high heat. Lightly brush with olive oil then griddle the sourdough bread for 1-2 minutes on each side until it has charred lines. Set aside until ready to serve.

6. When the mushrooms are cooked, spoon them onto the griddled sourdough and serve with a drizzle of olive oil.

PURPLE SPROUTING BROCCOLI WITH BEURRE NOISETTE & TOASTED ALMONDS

As a child, I always thought that broccoli was like little trees... a weird thought, but it made me eat lots of it! I still love broccoli and this is a great way to jazz up one of your 5-a-day. 'Beurre noisette' is the French name for burnt butter, which might sound like a strange thing to do, but adds a lovely rich, nutty finish to the dish.

SERVES 4 AS A SIDE

300g purple sprouting broccoli, ends trimmed
100ml chicken (or vegetable) stock
50g butter
25g toasted flaked almonds
Salt and pepper

1 Preheat the oven to 200°C/180°C fan/gas mark 6.

2 Measure out a piece of foil, 70cm x 30cm, and fold it in half into a near-square.

3 Open up the folded foil, arrange the broccoli in the middle of the bottom half and season with a little salt and pepper. Fold over the top half of the foil, then fold up two sides of the parcel, to seal, leaving one side open.

4 Pour the chicken stock into the parcel, and seal the final side so the whole parcel is closed. Place on a baking sheet and cook in the oven for 15 minutes.

5 While the broccoli is cooking, melt the butter in a saucepan and cook until it turns a dark brown or hazelnut colour (this is known as beurre noisette). Remove from the heat and set aside until ready to serve.

6 When the broccoli has cooked, open the parcel and use a slotted spoon to transfer the broccoli into a serving dish.

7 Drizzle the broccoli with the beurre noisette and scatter with the toasted almonds. Mix well with a spoon so everything is coated. Serve straightaway.

ENGLISH SUMMER GARDEN PARCEL with GOATS' CHEESE

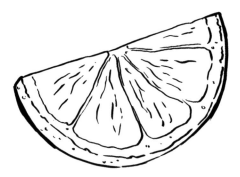

When I was growing up, we used to visit our family up north in Sunderland. My great-nan grew lots of veg – I'd go out in the garden with my sister and we'd pick all the fresh peas and gobble them up! This recipe reminds me of those times and includes many of the lovely ingredients I associate with summer.

SERVES 4 AS A SIDE

150g courgettes, sliced 5mm thick

75g tenderstem broccoli, halved lengthways

75g runner beans, finely sliced

75g freshly shelled peas

100g asparagus tips

Leaves from 3 thyme sprigs

Grated zest of 1 lemon, plus a squeeze of juice

Rapeseed oil, for drizzling

50ml vegetable stock

100g goats' cheese, rind removed

2 tbsp finely chopped mint

Salt and pepper

1 Preheat the oven to 180°C/160°C fan/gas mark 4.

2 Measure out a piece of parchment paper 70cm x 30cm, then fold it in half.

3 Open up the folded parchment square and arrange the courgettes, broccoli and runner beans in the middle of the bottom square of paper. Scatter with the shelled peas and asparagus tips.

4 Sprinkle with the thyme leaves and grate half the lemon zest over the top, then season with salt and pepper and drizzle with rapeseed oil.

5 Fold over the top half of the paper, then fold up two sides, to seal, leaving one side open. Pour the vegetable stock into the parcel, then seal up the final side so the whole parcel is closed.

6 Place onto a baking sheet and bake in the oven for 15 minutes. When it is ready, take the parcel out of the oven and open it. Grate over the remaining lemon zest and dress the vegetables with a squeeze of lemon juice.

7 Crumble the goats' cheese over the top and scatter with the mint. Drizzle with a little rapeseed oil and serve while hot.

COD WITH PESTO & PARMESAN CRUMBS

SERVES 4

FOR THE FISH

4 x cod loins (approx. 175g each)

30g panko breadcrumbs, or dried white breadcrumbs

20g Parmesan cheese, finely grated

Salt and pepper

FOR THE PESTO

1 bunch of basil (approx. 30g)

50g Parmesan cheese, grated

50g pine nuts

1 garlic clove, crushed

100ml olive oil

Squeeze of lemon juice

These parcels are full of flavour, with the cod standing up to the bold pesto, and the Parmesan crumbs adding a nice crunchy finish. You can even add herbs to the crumbs to pack in yet more flavour. Japanese panko breadcrumbs are good here because of their finer texture – look for them in the world foods section of the supermarket. This recipe also works with other meaty white fish, such as pollock or haddock.

1. Preheat the oven to 220°C/200°C fan/gas mark 7.

2. Start with the pesto. In a food processor, blitz the basil (including stalks), Parmesan, pine nuts, garlic and olive oil until you have a smooth purée. Add a squeeze of lemon juice and season with salt and pepper. Remove from the processor and empty into a bowl. Set aside until ready to use.

3. Measure out four rectangles of parchment paper, 50cm x 25cm, and fold each in half into a square.

4. Open up the folded parchment squares and place a cod loin in the middle of each of the bottom squares of paper. Season with salt and pepper, and spoon 2 tablespoons of pesto onto each piece of fish. Fold over the top half of the paper, then fold up the edges of each square to make into a parcel with the cod inside.

5. Place the parcels on a baking tray and bake in the oven for 15 minutes.

6. While the cod is cooking, put the breadcrumbs in a dry frying pan on a low-medium heat and toast for 1–2 minutes until golden, tossing occasionally. Pour into a mixing bowl and stir the Parmesan through the crumbs.

7. When the cod has cooked, remove from the oven and cut open the top of each bag. Sprinkle the Parmesan crumbs equally over the four portions and serve.

TIP Any remaining pesto can be kept in a jar in the fridge for up to 1 week, to serve with pasta.

GOOEY CHOCOLATE BANANAS

This dessert brings back memories of Bonfire Night with my mum, dad and sister. We would fill bananas with chocolate buttons and roast them on the barbecue while watching the fireworks. You can cook these in the oven or on the barbecue: either way it will transport you back to being a kid!

SERVES 4

4 large ripe bananas
100g chocolate buttons
2 oaty Hobnob biscuits or
    chocolate-chip cookies
Butter, for greasing
Vanilla Ice Cream (see
    page 224), to serve

1. Preheat the oven to 180°C/160°C fan/gas mark 4.

2. Peel the bananas and slice lengthways, but only three-quarters of the way down, then fill the cuts with the chocolate buttons.

3. Measure out four rectangles of foil, 40cm x 20cm, and then fold each in half into a square.

4. Open up the folded foil squares and smear each of the bottom squares with a little butter, then place a chocolate-filled banana in the middle. Fold over the top half of the foil and fold up the edges of the square to seal.

5. Place the parcels onto a baking tray and bake in the oven for 15 minutes.

6. Blitz the biscuits in a food processor until you have rough crumbs and set them aside until ready to serve.

7. When the bananas are ready, serve with the crumbled biscuits and a dollop of ice cream.

ROASTED STONE FRUIT WITH VANILLA MASCARPONE CREAM

Roasting fruits brings out their natural sugars and sweetness. You can give this recipe a twist by adding warming winter spices like star anise and cinnamon, or for a boozy kick why not add a splash of amaretto liqueur to the mascarpone cream?

SERVES 4

FOR THE FRUIT
2 peaches, halved and
    stones removed
2 nectarines, halved and
    stones removed
2 apricots, halved and
    stones removed
100g cherries, stalks and
    stones removed
1 tbsp vanilla paste
2 tbsp honey

FOR THE MASCARPONE CREAM
200g mascarpone cheese
    (remove from the fridge
    30 minutes in advance)
100ml double cream, plus
    a splash more if needed
1 tbsp vanilla paste
2 tbsp icing sugar

1 Preheat the oven to 200°C/180°C fan/gas mark 6.

2 Measure out a piece of parchment paper, 70cm x 25cm, and fold it in half.

3 Open up the folded parchment and arrange the fruit on the bottom half of the paper, then dot with vanilla paste and drizzle with the honey.

4 Fold over the top half of the paper, then fold up the edges to seal the parcel. Place it on a baking sheet and bake in the oven for 15–20 minutes.

5 While the fruit is roasting, make the vanilla mascarpone cream. In a mixing bowl, whisk all the ingredients until well combined. Set aside until ready to serve. If the mixture seems too thick add a little more double cream.

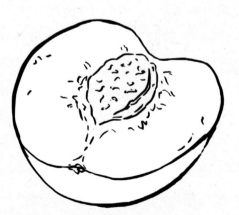

PIMP MY CORN!!!

MAKES 50G BAGS

50g popcorn kernels
Flavourings of choice (see opposite)

EQUIPMENT
1 x paper food bag

Who wouldn't want to pimp their corn!? These bags of badness are perfect for film nights at home. Get creative and invent your own flavour combos.

1 Put the popcorn kernels into the paper food bag and microwave for 1 minute 30 seconds to 3 minutes (depending on the power of your microwave).

2 Remove from the microwave and add flavourings (see opposite).

ROSEMARY SEA SALT

30g unsalted butter
1 tbsp finely chopped
    rosemary
Maldon sea salt or
    rosemary-infused salt

Melt the butter in a saucepan with the chopped rosemary and cook on a gentle heat for 1–2 minutes. This will infuse the butter. Strain the butter to remove the rosemary and leave to cool for 1–2 minutes. Pour the slightly cooled butter over the cooked popcorn in the bag and season with salt. Shake so everything is well coated.

TRUFFLED POPCORN

30g unsalted butter
1 tbsp truffle oil
Maldon sea salt

Melt the butter in a saucepan with the truffle oil. When melted, leave to cool for 1–2 minutes. Pour the slightly cooled butter over the cooked popcorn in the bag and season with salt. Shake so everything is well coated.

CARAMEL POPCORN

2 tbsp Caramel Sauce (see
    page 118)

Melt the caramel sauce in a saucepan and allow to cool for 5 minutes. Pour over the cooked popcorn in the bag and shake, so everything is well coated.

BACON MAPLE SYRUP

25g streaky bacon, chopped
    into 1cm dice
25g unsalted butter, plus
    extra for frying
2 tbsp maple syrup

Cook the bacon in a frying pan with a knob of butter, for 2–3 minutes until crisp. Remove and drain on kitchen paper.

Heat the butter and maple syrup in a small saucepan on a medium heat for 2–3 minutes until melted, then add the bacon. When the bacon is sticky, leave to cool for 1–2 minutes. Pour the slightly cooled mixture over the cooked popcorn in the bag and shake well.

AT THE FIRST GLIMPSE OF SUNSHINE, WE BRITS DRAG OUT THE BARBECUE

from the garage, clean off the rust (from it not being used too often!), and fire it up. There's nothing quite like the smell of barbecued meat invading the airspace to make you think to yourself, 'Hooray, summer is here...', only to wake up the next morning to the unwelcome, monotonous pattering of rain on your windows once more. Just like that, the British summer is over and the barbecue is relegated to its designated corner of the garage to rust again until the next rays of sunshine eventually grace our skies.

You may think I'm being terribly negative here, but the truth is that I wrote the recipes for this chapter, perfect for a glorious summer's day, holed up at my parents' house during a torrential rainstorm. Testing the recipes was interesting, huddled under an umbrella in their garden. However, when the delicious food hit the table (indoors of course!), it brightened up that rainy afternoon and the miserable weather was soon forgotten.

Barbecuing and griddling gives food a charred, smoky flavour that you can't get any other way, unless you go all mad professor and use expensive gadgets and gizmos. Even better, the recipes in this chapter are all really simple: it's just a matter of adding flavour, letting things marinate in a nice bath of goodness, and then putting the food on the barbecue. It's a nice social way of cooking, with very little fuss. And if you don't fancy cooking under an umbrella, but do fancy giving some of these recipes a bash, you can just as easily use a griddle pan in your kitchen – which means you can recreate my Jerk Chicken or my favourite Minted Lamb Chops come rain, snow or even gales!

PIRI-PIRI PRAWNS

SERVES 4–6

500g large raw tiger
   prawns, peeled
3 red chillies, finely sliced
1 red pepper, deseeded
   and cut into 1cm chunks
50ml olive oil
Grated zest of 1 lime,
   plus 1 lime cut into
   wedges to serve
1 garlic clove, minced
Salt and pepper

These prawns have all the fire you'd expect from piri-piri, so they're not for the faint-hearted! They are so easy to make and certain to be a crowd pleaser.

1. Using a sharp knife, remove the black digestive tract from the prawns.

2. In a food processor, blitz all the ingredients, except for the prawns, and season with salt and pepper. Place the prawns in a baking tray with a rim, pour over the marinade and leave for 2 hours.

3. When you are ready to cook, light the barbecue or preheat the grill. Slide the prawns onto metal skewers and grill for 2–3 minutes on each side, until the prawns turn pink.

4. Remove from the skewers and serve with lime wedges.

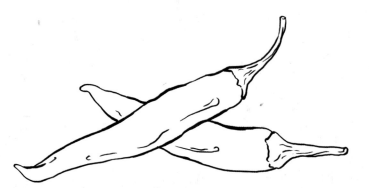

GRIDDLED TUNA with TOMATOES, BASIL & LEMON

This recipe is super-healthy and super-quick, so it's perfect for when you're watching those calories or you want a meal on the fly. It can be made in just 10 minutes, yet tastes like you've spent hours preparing it.

SERVES 4

20 baby vine tomatoes, cut into bunches of 5 but kept on the vine
4 tbsp olive oil, plus extra for drizzling
4 tuna steaks (approx. 150g each)
Grated zest and juice of 1 lemon, plus lemon wedges to serve
10 basil leaves, finely sliced, plus a few sprigs to garnish
Salt and pepper

1 In a mixing bowl, drizzle the tomatoes with a little olive oil and season with salt and pepper.

2 Heat a griddle pan on a high hob until very hot. Add the tomatoes, each bunch still on the vine, cooking them for 4–5 minutes until they start to blister.

3 While the tomatoes are cooking, drizzle a little olive oil on the tuna steaks and rub it all over. Season with salt and pepper. Remove the tomatoes from the heat and keep warm until ready to serve. Place the tuna steaks on the hot griddle pan and cook for about 2 minutes each side, until white on the outside with char marks, but still pink on the inside.

4 Remove from the pan and place on a plate. Add the tomatoes, still on the vine, to the plate.

5 Mix the 4 tablespoons of olive oil, the lemon zest and juice and the basil, and season with a little salt. Use this to dress the tuna and tomatoes, then garnish with sprigs of basil and serve with lemon wedges.

TANDOORI CHICKEN WITH RAITA

My dad absolutely loves tandoori chicken done on a barbecue, so I've included this recipe especially for him. I've paired it with a cooling yoghurt raita to tame the fiery taste.

SERVES 4

FOR THE CHICKEN

8 chicken thighs or
   drumsticks, with skin
2 tbsp chopped fresh
   coriander, to serve

FOR THE MARINADE

200ml buttermilk
200ml yoghurt
2 cloves, ground
1 tbsp tandoori masala
   powder
1 tbsp garam masala
1 tsp cayenne pepper
1 tsp ground cumin
1 tsp paprika
1 tsp ground coriander
Juice of 1 lime
1 medium onion, grated
Salt and pepper

FOR THE RAITA

200g natural yoghurt
½ cucumber, peeled, deseeded
   and grated
Juice of ½ lemon
Leaves from 4 mint sprigs,
   finely chopped
½ tsp ground cumin

1 Using a small knife, criss-cross the chicken skin, which allows the marinade to penetrate the meat.

2 Mix all of the marinade ingredients together in a bowl and stir well. Season with salt and pepper. Place the chicken in a large food/freezer bag (or use a couple if yours are smaller) and pour in the marinade. Seal the bag/s and massage the marinade into the chicken. Leave to infuse for a minimum of 2 hours, preferably overnight.

3 When you are ready to cook, preheat the oven to 180°C/160°C fan/gas mark 4 and light your barbecue, if using.

4 Place the chicken pieces into a roasting tin, spoon over half of the marinade (reserve the remainder), and cook in the oven for 20 minutes.

5 Meanwhile, put all the raita ingredients into a mixing bowl and stir well. Season with a pinch of salt and set aside in the fridge until ready to serve.

6 Remove the chicken from the oven, to finish cooking on the barbecue or, alternatively, on a griddle pan over a hot hob. Grill or griddle for 4–5 minutes on each side, until beginning to blacken. Keep an eye on it as it can burn quickly. If the chicken starts to look dry, brush with the reserved marinade to keep it nice and juicy.

7 To check the chicken is cooked all the way through, pierce it with a skewer: if the juices run clear, then it is ready. If not, give it a little more time and then test again.

8 Remove from the barbecue or pan and serve with the chopped coriander scattered on top and the raita on the side.

COWBOY RIBS
XXXXXXXX

When I was a teenager we went on holiday to Florida and I remember eating some of the best ribs ever. The Americans certainly know how to do them, and this recipe for sweet, smoky and addictive cowboy ribs really takes me back. You can imagine Desperate Dan tucking into these bad boys!

SERVES 2–4

2 x racks of baby back pork ribs

FOR THE MARINADE
2 garlic cloves, peeled and crushed
4cm piece of ginger, peeled and grated
150ml tomato ketchup
150ml honey
150ml apple juice
3 tbsp Worcestershire sauce
2 tbsp smoked paprika
4 whole star anise
2 bay leaves
4 tbsp Dijon mustard
Salt and pepper

1 Put all the marinade ingredients in a mixing bowl and whisk together well. Season with salt and pepper.

2 Lay the racks of ribs in a roasting tray. Pour two thirds of the marinade over the ribs, coating them evenly. Reserve the remaining marinade in the fridge until ready to cook. Leave the ribs to marinate for a minimum of 2 hours, preferably overnight.

3 When ready to cook, preheat the oven to 160°C/140°C fan/gas mark 3.

4 Cook the ribs in the oven for 1 hour, basting every 15 minutes to make sure that the marinade doesn't burn on the bottom of the roasting tin and to keep the ribs juicy and moist. Towards the end of the cooking time, light the barbecue or heat a griddle pan over a high heat.

5 Remove the ribs from the oven, to finish cooking on the barbecue for a nice smoky flavour. Barbecue or griddle for 7-10 minutes on each side, until beginning to blacken. Using a pastry brush, cover the ribs with the reserved marinade as they are cooking, to make sure they have a nice sticky coating.

6 Once cooked, remove the ribs and serve while still hot.

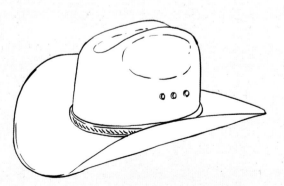

MEXICAN STEAK WITH SALSA

SERVES 4

FOR THE STEAK
4 sirloin steaks (approx.
    220g each)
8 plain or soft corn
    tortillas, to serve

FOR THE MARINADE
½ tsp chipotle powder or
    1 tsp chipotle paste
2 garlic cloves, peeled
    and crushed
1 tsp ground cumin
1 tsp paprika
1 tsp oregano
1 tsp coriander seeds
1 tbsp olive oil
Salt and pepper

FOR THE SALSA
250g cherry tomatoes
½ red onion, finely sliced
3 tbsp roughly chopped
    coriander
1 red chilli, finely chopped
Grated zest and juice of
    1 lime

My Mexican steak is a nice take on fajitas and great served with a fresh, vibrant salsa and soft tortilla wraps. It's quick and easy, and delivers lots of flavour. Chipotle powder is used a lot in Mexican and Tex-Mex cooking. It's made from smoked chillies, so it adds a delicious smoky note to the meat. Some supermarkets sell chipotle paste, so you can use that instead if you can't get hold of the powder.

1. Using a pestle and mortar, mix all the marinade ingredients together until you have a smooth paste.

2. Put the steaks into a large food/freezer bag (or use a couple if yours are smaller) and pour in the marinade. Seal the bag/s and massage well so the meat is thoroughly coated with the marinade. Leave to infuse for a minimum of 2 hours, preferably overnight.

3. To make the salsa, chop the tomatoes into eighths and mix with the onion, coriander, chilli, lime zest and juice. You can make this ahead of time and leave it at room temperature until needed, but only add the lime juice at the very last minute.

4. When you are ready to cook, light the barbecue or preheat the grill. Grill the steaks for 3–4 minutes on each side, then leave to rest for 5 minutes. Cut into 1cm slices and serve with the salsa and warmed tortillas.

minted LAMB CHOPS

SERVES 4

8 lamb loin chops, (80–100g each)
Leaves from 6 mint sprigs, finely chopped, plus extra to serve
1 tbsp dried mint
2 garlic cloves, crushed
1 tbsp honey
Olive oil
Salt and pepper

One of my favourite things to eat in the world is a minted lamb chop, cooked on the barbecue. I love the smell of it cooking, that minty-fresh flavour with the meat, and the way the fat goes super-crispy! Any time my parents do a barbecue I always insist that we have minted lamb chops. Here's my simple recipe for them.

1 Put the lamb chops into a large food/freezer bag (or use a couple if yours are smaller). Add the fresh mint, dried mint, garlic, honey and a good glug of olive oil to the bag/s. Season with salt and pepper, then seal the bag/s and massage the lamb chops, so they are fully coated in the minty marinade.

2 Leave to infuse for a minimum of 2 hours, preferably overnight. The longer you leave it, the more flavour the lamb takes on.

3 When you are ready to cook, light the barbecue or preheat the grill. Grill the chops for 4–5 minutes on each side, until cooked through and golden or crispy on the outside.

4 Leave to rest for 5 minutes before serving, scattered with chopped fresh mint.

CHARRED ROSEMARY & ORANGE MACKEREL

SERVES 4

4 whole mackerel, cleaned
    and gills removed
Olive oil, for drizzling
Leaves from 2 rosemary
    sprigs, roughly chopped
2 oranges
Salt and pepper

EQUIPMENT
Wire grilling cage for fish
    (optional)

I love the combo of rosemary and orange, which works beautifully with mackerel – sometimes the simple things in life are best. When buying mackerel, look for fish with bright or deep-red gills, clear eyes, and flesh that is bright and shiny, not greying. It's easiest to ask the fishmonger to gut the fish for you and remove the gills.

1 Score 4–5 cuts on both sides of each mackerel using a small paring knife. This allows the marinade to penetrate the fish. Lay the mackerel in a baking tray (ideally one with a rim) and drizzle with a good glug of olive oil. Season with salt and pepper, and scatter with the chopped rosemary.

2 Using a grater or microplane, grate the zest from one of the oranges over the top of the mackerel. Rub the zest and rosemary all over the fish, into the cuts and the insides. Set aside to marinate for a minimum of 2 hours, or preferably in the fridge overnight.

3 When you are ready to cook, light the barbecue or heat a griddle pan over a medium–high heat. Cut the other orange into four thin slices and put one slice inside each mackerel.

4 If you have a wire grilling cage, put the mackerel inside and place on the barbecue to cook for 3–4 minutes on each side, until blackened/charred on the outside and the flesh is firm and cooked through – it should have turned white and opaque. If you do not have a grilling cage, wrap the fish in foil and cook for the same amount of time. If using a griddle, place the mackerel directly in the pan and cook for about 4 minutes on each side.

5 Remove the mackerel from the cage or foil and serve with a drizzle of olive oil.

JERK CHICKEN

SERVES 4

8 chicken thighs or
    drumsticks, with skin

FOR THE MARINADE
1 tbsp dark brown sugar
1 bunch of spring onions,
    topped and tailed and
    roughly chopped
3 Scotch bonnet chillies
    (seeds removed if you
    want less fire)
3 tbsp soy sauce
1 tbsp dried thyme
½ nutmeg, grated
1 tsp ground cinnamon
½ tsp ground allspice
4 tbsp honey
3cm piece of ginger,
    peeled and grated
Grated zest of 1 orange
1 tsp black peppercorns
200ml orange juice

Around where I live in East London, street food is massive, and jerk chicken is always a winner with me and my mates. My take on jerk isn't as hot as the Jamaicans probably like it, but it still has a kick to it! Serve with rice and peas (in Caribbean food this means kidney beans not green peas), and roasted sweet potatoes.

1 Blitz all of the marinade ingredients, except for the orange juice, in a food processor until you have a smooth mixture. Add the orange juice and pulse again until well mixed.

2 Using a small knife, criss-cross the chicken skin, which allows the meat to take on more flavour from the marinade, then place the chicken in a large food/freezer bag (or use a couple if yours are smaller) and pour in the marinade. Seal the bag/s and massage the marinade into the chicken. Leave to infuse for a minimum of 4 hours, preferably overnight.

3 When ready to cook, preheat the oven to 180°C/160°C fan/ gas mark 4 and light your barbecue, if using.

4 Place the chicken pieces into a roasting tin and spoon over half of the marinade (reserve the remaining), and bake for 20 minutes.

5 Remove from the oven, to finish cooking on the barbecue or, alternatively, in a griddle pan on a hot hob. Grill or griddle for 4–5 minutes on each side, until the chicken skin begins to blacken. Keep an eye on it as it can burn quickly. If the meat starts to look dry, brush with the reserved marinade to keep it nice and juicy.

6 To check the chicken is cooked all the way through, pierce it with a skewer: if the juices run clear then it is ready. If not, give it a little more time and then test again.

7 Remove from the barbecue or pan and serve straightaway.

GRIDDLED HARISSA HALLOUMI with COUSCOUS

SERVES 4

FOR THE HALLOUMI

400g halloumi cheese, cut into 1cm-thick slices
2 tbsp harissa paste
1 tbsp olive oil

FOR THE COUSCOUS

200g cherry tomatoes
1 tbsp olive oil, plus extra for drizzling and dressing
1 medium onion, finely diced
300ml chicken (or vegetable) stock
200g dried couscous
200g roasted red peppers from a jar, drained and cut into 1cm dice
4 tbsp finely chopped parsley
4 tbsp finely chopped coriander
50g toasted flaked almonds
Juice of 1 lemon
½ tsp sumac (optional)
Salt and pepper

TO SERVE (OPTIONAL)

100ml natural yoghurt
1 red chilli, finely sliced
2 tbsp chopped coriander

Harissa is a hot chilli paste that delivers a blast of North-African heat, so serve this dish with the yoghurt if you want something on hand to cool it down. I also use a spice called sumac, a red/purple powder with a lemony flavour, which is common in Middle-Eastern cooking. It's not essential but it does add an extra dimension of seasoning to the couscous.

1 Put the halloumi in a mixing bowl, add the harissa paste and olive oil and mix well. Leave to marinate in the fridge for at least 2 hours, preferably overnight.

2 When ready to cook, preheat the oven to 200°C/180°C fan/gas mark 6.

3 Place the tomatoes into a small roasting tin, drizzle with olive oil and season with salt. Roast in the oven for 10 minutes until their skins have blistered. Remove and allow to cool slightly, then roughly chop into quarters and set aside.

4 Heat the tablespoon of olive oil in a frying pan on a medium heat, and cook the onion for 3 minutes until translucent and soft, but don't let it brown. Remove from the heat and set aside.

5 Heat the stock in a saucepan until nearly boiling. Place the couscous in a large mixing bowl, pour in the hot stock, mix with a fork and cover with cling film. Leave to stand for 10 minutes then run a fork through the couscous to break up the grains and stop it becoming one big lump.

6 Add the tomatoes, peppers (and any juice released when chopping them), fried onion, parsley, coriander, flaked almonds, lemon juice and sumac (if using) to the couscous, and mix well so everything is distributed evenly. Dress with 3-4 tablespoons of olive oil, to your taste. Season with salt and pepper, but just lightly as stock tends to be salty already. Cover with cling film to keep warm and set aside until ready to serve.

7 Heat a large griddle pan on a hot hob until nearly smoking, then griddle the halloumi slices for 2-3 minutes on each side until they have nice brown griddle lines on them. Remove from the heat and season with salt and pepper.

8 To serve, spoon the couscous into bowls and place the halloumi on top. If you like, serve with the chilli and coriander, and a dollop of natural yoghurt to cool the heat.

CHARGRILLED ROMANESCO SALAD

Romanesco is a great-looking vegetable. In fact, it looks like it comes from Mars! It's from the cauliflower family, and although it's not something you see every day, it is gradually creeping into our supermarkets. The textures in this dish all work really well together. I love the crunch from the hazelnuts and the sweetness of the raisins and orange. This makes a good side for pork or fish, or a humble main course on its own.

SERVES 6 (AS A SIDE)

1 large Romanesco cauliflower, cut into small florets
1 bulb of red or white chicory (approx. 100g)
1 tsp sherry vinegar
½ head of radicchio (approx. 120g), finely shredded
30g sultanas or raisins
Grated zest of ¼ orange, plus a squeeze of juice
30g whole blanched hazelnuts
¼ white cauliflower, finely sliced on a mandolin or with a knife
Olive oil
Salt

FOR THE DRESSING
1 tbsp hazelnut oil
1 tbsp sherry vinegar
1 tbsp groundnut oil

1. Heat a griddle pan on a medium-high hob until nearly smoking.

2. Place the Romanesco florets in a mixing bowl, drizzle with olive oil and mix together well. Cook them on the griddle pan for about 2 minutes on each side until charred. Set aside on a plate, leaving the griddle on the hob.

3. In the mixing bowl, toss the chicory leaves with more olive oil and season with salt. Cook for 1–2 minutes on the griddle pan, so that the leaves wilt and get slight char marks. Return them to the mixing bowl and dress with the sherry vinegar. Mix well.

4. In another bowl, mix the radicchio and raisins with olive oil and a squeeze of orange juice (reserving the zest).

5. Toast the hazelnuts in a dry frying pan over a low heat until golden, tossing occasionally, then roughly crush them in a pestle and mortar.

6. Place all the ingredients on a large serving dish and sprinkle over the raw white cauliflower slices. Whisk together all the ingredients for the dressing, season with salt and pour it over. Finish with the grated orange zest.

GRIDDLED AUBERGINE BAKE

**SERVES 4 AS A MAIN, OR
6 AS A SIDE**

3 large aubergines, tops
   removed and flesh cut
   lengthways into 1cm slices
   (about 21 slices total)
Olive oil
Salt and pepper

FOR THE FILLING
1 large onion, finely diced
100g feta cheese, crumbled
150g ricotta
1 tbsp oregano
2 tbsp finely sliced mint
2 tbsp finely chopped dill
1 red chilli, deseeded and
   finely chopped
Grated zest of ½ lemon
100g cherry tomatoes, cut
   into eighths

FOR THE TOPPING
1 egg yolk, beaten
200g Greek yoghurt
50g Parmesan cheese,
   grated

**This is a perfect bake for meat-free Mondays or any time
you fancy a veggie dinner. The hearty aubergine and
feta cheese certainly fills the void. If you want this to go
a bit further, serve with a big Greek salad. It also works
well as a side dish for roasted lamb.**

1 Preheat the oven to 200°C/180°C fan/gas mark 6. Heat a large
griddle pan on a medium-high hob.

2 Place the aubergine slices in a bowl, drizzle with olive oil and
season with salt and pepper.

3 In batches, griddle the aubergine slices for 4–5 minutes on
each side until cooked through and charred on both sides,
placing the finished batches on a wire rack as they are
removed from the pan.

4 Add a little olive oil to a frying pan on a medium heat, and
soften the onion for the filling for 3 minutes until tender.
Set aside to cool slightly.

5 In a large bowl, mix the remaining filling ingredients with
the cooled onions and season with a little salt and pepper.

6 Lay one aubergine slice flat and spoon 1 tablespoon of the
filling onto its 'fat' end. Gently roll it up, then place into a
baking dish about 30cm x 25cm and 5cm deep. Do the same
for the rest of the aubergine slices and filling. You want them
to fill the dish without any gaps.

7 In another bowl, whisk the egg yolk, yoghurt and Parmesan
and season with a little salt and pepper. Spoon on top of the
aubergine rolls and spread evenly over the surface. Bake in
the oven for 35–40 minutes until the topping is golden and
set. Serve straightaway.

PINEAPPLE KEBABS WITH → RUM GLAZE

SERVES 4–6

1 large pineapple, peeled
    and cored, eyes removed
    and cut into 6 wedges/
    slices

FOR THE GLAZE
15g unsalted butter
3 tbsp pineapple juice
2 tbsp dark rum
Grated zest and juice of
    ½ lime
2 tbsp honey

EQUIPMENT
6 x 30cm-long wooden
    skewers

If you close your eyes and take a bite, you might imagine you're on a sunny Caribbean beach... The cheeky rum glaze means these kebabs aren't for the kids, but grown-ups definitely won't struggle to polish them off! This recipe also works well with mango if you want to mix it up.

 Soak the wooden skewers in water for 30 minutes.

2 Light the barbecue or put a griddle pan on the hob over a high heat.

3 Place all the glaze ingredients in a saucepan with 1 tablespoon of water and melt together over a low heat for 1–2 minutes, then simmer for 1–2 minutes. Remove from the heat and set aside.

4 Skewer the pineapple wedges and, using a pastry brush, lightly brush them with the glaze.

5 Cook on the barbecue or griddle pan for 2–3 minutes on each side, basting with more glaze as they cook, until the pineapple is caramelised and has char marks. Remove from the heat and serve warm.

TIP Once the pineapple is skewered, wrap the exposed ends of the wooden skewers in foil, to stop them from burning on the barbecue or griddle pan.

BRIOCHE SOLDIERS WITH CHOCOLATE DIPPING SAUCE

Everyone loves a boiled egg with soldiers, so here's my dessert version, minus the egg...! Chocolate is said to trigger the happy hormones, so this is the ultimate indulgence to get you feeling good. It's very rich, so is nice served with strawberries to add some freshness.

SERVES 4

FOR THE SOLDIERS
8 slices of brioche (from a 400g loaf)
Knob of butter
300g strawberries, to serve

FOR THE CHOCOLATE DIPPING SAUCE
100g dark chocolate, broken into pieces
100ml double cream
1 tbsp vanilla paste
2 tbsp honey

1. Put all the ingredients for the chocolate sauce in a saucepan and place on a medium heat for 2-3 minutes until melted. When the chocolate mixture begins to thicken, remove from the heat and pour into ramekins or small serving dishes.

2. Heat a griddle pan on a medium-high hob. Add a knob of butter, then griddle the brioche slices in batches for 20-30 seconds on each side until they get char marks.

3. Remove from the pan and cut into soldiers. Serve with the warm dipping sauce and strawberries.

PEACHES WITH GRANOLA YOGHURT & HONEY

This quick and simple breakfast recipe is a great alternative to a bowl of cereal. Chargrilling the peaches brings out their natural sugars, which means lots of extra flavour to go alongside the tangy yoghurt and sweet honey.

SERVES 4

Vegetable oil, for brushing
4 ripe peaches, halved and
   de-stoned
300g natural yoghurt
Juice of ½ lemon
80g granola
8 fresh mint leaves, finely
   sliced (optional)
4 tsp honey

1 Heat a griddle pan on a medium–high hob and brush with vegetable oil.

2 Lay the peaches skin-side down on the hot griddle pan and cook for 2–3 minutes, until they have nice char marks but are still firm. Don't disturb them while cooking, or you will not get the char marks. Turn over and cook for a further 2–3 minutes on the other side.

3 While the peaches are cooking, place the yoghurt in a bowl and mix in the lemon juice.

4 When the peaches are cooked on both sides, remove from the heat and serve with the yoghurt and granola, scattered with mint, if using, and drizzled with honey.

THE FIRST TIME I CAME ACROSS SALT BAKING WAS ON *MASTERCHEF.*

I had never seen this technique used before but suddenly I was thrown in at the deep end and asked to cook with a salt-crust pastry for a group of three-Michelin-starred chefs, under the watchful eye of Simon Rogan.

There are several different methods of baking in salt, including cooking food completely encased in salt or baking it in salted pastry. The purpose? The crust or pastry case traps in all the moisture, so the cooked ingredient ends up moist and beautifully juicy, especially good for large pieces of meat or fish that otherwise tend to dry out. The food also gets seasoned as it cooks and infused with any flavours you've incorporated into the crust, such as herbs or spices (so feel free to experiment and adapt things to your own taste). The salt crust or pastry itself doesn't get eaten – it's only used for cooking, and is removed and thrown away before serving, or can be cracked open at the table if you want to make things more dramatic for your dinner guests.

Another simple method is to cook food directly on a layer of salt. This acts as a barrier between the heat and the food, to help avoid it scorching or sticking, and again seasons the food as it cooks. I've used this trick in my Spanish Pil-Pil Prawns recipe and for some amazing Salted Baked Potatoes.

I came across salt baking again while doing a 'stage' (yet another posh French word, meaning work experience in a professional kitchen) at Tom Kerridge's pub The Hand and Flowers. I discovered that many of the best restaurants use this technique, but even though it was alien to me, I soon realised what a simple process it is and definitely something that's achievable at home. So give it a go – the salt does all the hard work and your guests are guaranteed to be impressed when you say to them: 'Tonight, we have salt-baked... on the menu'!

SALT-BAKED BEETROOT SALAD WITH MOZZARELLA & HAZELNUTS

Baking beetroots in a salt crust is something I learned when working at Tom Kerridge's pub The Hand and Flowers. I spent many hours in the prep kitchen learning new techniques alongside a future food rockstar chef, Connor. At 16 he is working in a two-star kitchen and could probably run rings around chefs twice his age. He told me that salt-baking is an amazing way of cooking beets as it really brings out the flavour. They go well with the creamy mozzarella, or you can swap in goats' cheese or ricotta if you fancy a stronger flavour.

SERVES 4–6

FOR THE SALAD

4 large mixed beetroots (golden/purple/candy), unpeeled
25g hazelnuts, shelled and peeled
3 x 125g balls of mozzarella
50g mixed salad leaves (baby chard/lamb's lettuce/rocket)
Leaves from 1 sprig of thyme
Grated zest of ⅓ orange
Olive oil
Salt and pepper

FOR THE SALT-CRUST PASTRY

450g coarse sea salt
750g plain flour, plus extra for dusting
450ml warm water

FOR THE DRESSING

2 tbsp groundnut oil
2 tbsp hazelnut oil
2 tbsp sherry vinegar

1. Preheat the oven to 180°C/160°C fan/gas mark 4.

2. First, make the salt-crust pastry. In a large bowl, mix the salt and flour and gradually mix in the warm water.

3. Work into a rough dough, then turn tout onto a floured work surface and knead for 5 minutes until everything is mixed well and you have a smooth dough.

4. Divide the dough into four balls and roll out one at a time into rough squares large enough to encase each beetroot. Place one beet in the first square of dough and fold up the edges so the beetroot is completely encased and there are no gaps. Do the same for the other beets.

5. Place onto a baking sheet lined with parchment paper, and bake for 1 hour 30 to 1 hour 45 minutes. To test whether they are ready, insert a skewer through the pastry and into the heart of a beetroot – if it goes in without too much resistance and feels tender, it is ready.

6. Remove from the oven and let them rest in the pastry for 10 minutes, then remove and discard the pastry crust.

 CONTINUES

CONTINUED

7   Peel the beetroots under a running tap. Cut them into eight wedges. Set aside until ready to serve.

8   Now prepare the rest of the salad. Toast the hazelnuts for 2–3 minutes over a medium heat in a dry pan, then place in a pestle and mortar and lightly crush. Set aside.

9   Tear the mozzarella into pieces and drizzle with a little olive oil. Season with a crack of black pepper and salt. Set aside.

10 For the dressing, whisk all the ingredients in a bowl and season with salt.

11 To serve, arrange three or four beetroot wedges and a handful of salad leaves on each plate. Scatter half the hazelnuts, thyme leaves and mozzarella equally across all the plates. Repeat with another three or four beetroot wedges and a handful of salad leaves per plate, scatter with the remaining hazelnuts, thyme and mozzarella, then grate over the orange zest and drizzle with the dressing.

SEA BREAM with SAUCE VIERGE

SERVES 2

FOR THE SEA BREAM
2 x 400g sea bream, gutted
2kg coarse sea salt
½ lemon, sliced (or enough to
    fill the cavities of the fish)
2 sprigs of basil

FOR THE SAUCE VIERGE
½ tsp coriander seeds
2 plum tomatoes
100ml olive oil
Juice from ½ lemon
1 shallot, finely diced
2 tbsp chopped basil
Salt and pepper

Baking fish in a salt crust keeps the flesh beautifully juicy and looks very impressive when entertaining guests as it can be brought to the table whole and still in its crust. The sauce can be made earlier in the afternoon and then gently reheated or served at room temperature.

 Preheat the oven to 220°C/200°C fan/gas mark 7.

 First, make the sauce vierge. This can be made ahead of time and served at room temperature, or gently reheated. Toast the coriander seeds in a small dry frying pan on a gentle heat for 1–2 minutes until they release their flavour. Tip into a pestle and mortar and roughly crush.

 Put the kettle on to boil. Using a sharp knife, make a small cross on the top of each tomato and place in a bowl. Pour enough boiling water over the tomatoes to cover and leave them for 1–2 minutes until the skins start to peel away. Plunge into a separate bowl of cold water, peel off all the skin and discard. Cut each tomato into quarters, remove the seeds and discard, and cut the flesh into fine dice.

 Gently warm the olive oil in a saucepan for 2–3 minutes on a low heat. You don't want it to boil, just to be warmed through. Remove from the heat and add all the remaining ingredients, season with a good crack of pepper and salt, and leave to infuse for 20–30 minutes.

 Now prepare the bream. In a bowl, mix the salt with 250ml of water. Put the lemon slices and one sprig of basil into each bream's cavity.

 Pour about a quarter to a third of the salt in a layer at the bottom of a roasting tin and place the sea bream on top. Pour the remaining salt over the bream, then press all the salt (that isn't directly underneath the fish) up to and around the fish so they are completely encased with tightly packed salt. Make sure every part is covered. Cook in the oven for 20 minutes.

 When cooked, remove and let it stand for 5 minutes, then crack open the salt crust and discard. Peel the skin off the fish, gently remove the flesh and serve with the sauce vierge.

SALTED BAKED POTATOES *WITH* GARLIC & PARSLEY BUTTER

SERVES 4 AS A SIDE

800g coarse sea salt
800g baby or new potatoes
4 sprigs of rosemary
Bulb of garlic, cut into
    half horizontally
Olive oil
50g butter
1 tbsp finely chopped
    parsley
Pepper

Cooking potatoes on a layer of salt helps season them perfectly as they cook. Just make sure you brush off any excess salt grains stuck to them before you serve, or they might taste too salty. When roasted, garlic becomes gorgeously sweet, so it makes a delicious finishing touch when mixed with the butter and parsley.

1 Preheat the oven to 200°C/180°C fan/gas mark 6. Pour the salt into a roasting tin in an even layer.

2 Place the potatoes on top of the salt and add the sprigs of rosemary. Lightly brush the tops of the garlic bulb halves with a little olive oil and add facing upwards. Cover with foil and cook for 45 minutes.

3 Remove from the oven and set the garlic aside. Drizzle the potatoes with a good glug of olive oil and return to the oven for a further 20–25 minutes to cook uncovered.

4 Meanwhile, squeeze the garlic out of its skin and, using a spoon, smooth into a paste.

5 In a saucepan set over a low heat, melt the butter, then add the garlic and cook for 1–2 minutes until the butter and garlic are well combined. Remove from the heat and add the parsley. Set aside until ready to serve.

6 When the potato cooking time is up, test whether they are cooked all the way through with a knife.

7 Once cooked, remove the potatoes from the oven, lift them out of the salt, brush off any excess and place in a serving dish.

8 Pour over the garlic/herb butter and season with pepper, mix well and serve.

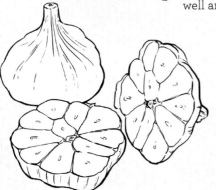

PIL-PIL PRAWNS with GREMOLATA

Don't be put off by the name here. It sounds pretty posh but in fact it's a simple Spanish dish of sizzling prawns with a herby garnish. It's fast and easy to make, yet looks and tastes super-impressive. I have a huge addiction to watching cookery programmes, and it was on TV that I first saw a chef cooking prawns on a bed of salt like this. The salt acts as a barrier between the food and the pan, helping to avoid sticking and burning, and also seasons the food as it cooks.

SERVES 4

FOR THE PRAWNS
2 x handfuls of Maldon
    sea salt
500g large raw tiger
    prawns, head and
    shells on
Olive oil
Big squeeze of lemon juice

FOR THE GREMOLATA
Grated zest of 2 lemons
2 tbsp finely chopped
    parsley
2 garlic cloves, grated

1 Make the gremolata first. Mix all the ingredients in a small bowl and set aside until ready to serve.

2 Heat two large frying pans over a medium to high heat. (You could do it in two batches, but that would mean washing up and drying a hot pan before starting all over again, so it's best to use two pans.) When hot, throw a handful of Maldon sea salt into each pan and let it heat for a further minute. You want the salt to be hot. Be careful, it may start to pop/spit.

3 When the salt is hot, place the prawns directly onto the salt and cook for 2–3 minutes until you see the underside turn a pink colour. When it's pink, use tongs to flip the prawns over and cook the other side for 2 minutes.

4 After 2 minutes, drizzle a good glug of olive oil over the prawns. They will sizzle and may give off some smoke. Cook for 1 more minute until completely pink, then remove and put onto a serving platter.

5 Sprinkle with the gremolata and drizzle with olive oil and a big squeeze of lemon juice.

SEA BASS SALSA VERDE

SERVES 4

1.5kg sea bass, gutted

FOR THE SALT CRUST
2kg coarse sea salt
3 tbsp fennel seeds,
  roughly ground with a
  pestle and mortar or
  spice blender
½ lemon, sliced

FOR THE SALSA VERDE
10g chives
15g parsley
7.5g mint
10g dill
Grated zest of ½ lemon
Juice of 1 lemon
6 anchovies
2 tsp capers, rinsed
½ red onion, diced
1 tsp Dijon mustard
1 garlic clove, peeled
100ml olive oil
Salt and pepper

This recipe is certainly one for impressing dinner guests. If you want a large sea bass, you may have to order it in advance from your local fishmonger, or you can always use smaller fishes if you prefer. The salsa verde can be prepared ahead of time as it keeps for a few days in the fridge.

1 Preheat the oven to 220°C/200°C fan/gas mark 7.

2 In a bowl, mix the salt and fennel seeds with 250ml of water. Put the lemon into the cavity of the sea bass.

3 Pour about a quarter to a third of the salt in a layer at the bottom of a roasting tin and place the sea bass on top. Pour the remaining salt over the sea bass, then press all the salt (that isn't directly underneath it) up to and around the fish so it is completely encased with tightly packed salt. Make sure every part is covered. Cook in the oven for 40 minutes.

4 Meanwhile, make the salsa verde. Place all of the ingredients into a food processor and blend until you have a smooth purée or sauce. Season with salt and pepper and set aside until ready to serve.

5 When the fish is cooked, remove it from the oven and let it stand for 5 minutes, then crack open the salt crust and discard. Peel the skin off the fish and gently remove the flesh. Serve with the salsa verde.

TIP To check if the fish is cooked through, insert the tip of a sharp knife into the centre of the flesh, remove and carefully touch it – if it's hot the fish is ready.

SALT-BAKED CARROTS WITH HERBY LENTILS

SERVES 4

FOR THE CARROTS

8 heritage carrots (purple,
    white, yellow, orange),
    stalks removed, scrubbed
250ml natural yoghurt
Juice of ½ lemon
2 tbsp finely chopped
    coriander, to serve
Olive oil
Salt and pepper

FOR THE SALT-CRUST
PASTRY

1 tbsp coriander seeds
1 tbsp cumin seeds
1 tbsp fennel seeds
600g coarse sea salt
1kg plain flour, plus extra for
    dusting
600ml warm water

FOR THE HERBY LENTILS

½ tsp coriander seeds
½ tsp cumin seeds
1 medium onion, finely
    diced
1 carrot, peeled and finely
    diced
1 celery stick, stringy bits
    removed and flesh finely
    diced
1 tbsp olive oil, plus extra
    for dressing
250g dried Puy lentils
300ml chicken (or
    vegetable) stock
4 tbsp finely chopped
    parsley

This is a great recipe for your veggie friends. I love using different-coloured carrots – you don't see them every day in the supermarkets but you can usually pick them up at your local greengrocer. It's also a good trick for getting kids to eat their veg, as the colours are fun and inviting. These herby, spiced lentils are the perfect partner, adding a contrasting taste and texture to the sweet, mellow carrots.

1 Preheat the oven to 200°C/180°C fan/gas mark 6.

2 First, make the salt-crust pastry. In a dry frying pan, toast the spices for 1–2 minutes until they release their flavour, then grind to a powder in a pestle and mortar.

3 In a large bowl, mix the salt, toasted and ground spices and flour and gradually mix in the warm water. Work into a rough dough, then turn the dough out onto a floured work surface and knead for 5 minutes until everything is mixed well and you have a smooth dough.

4 Divide the pastry into two balls, then roll out each ball to a rectangle 35cm x 20cm, the thickness of a pound coin. Put one of the pastry sheets into a large lightly greased roasting tin and arrange the carrots evenly on top, spreading them out, then cover with the other pastry sheet, sealing so there are no gaps and everything is encased.

5 Bake in the oven for 45 minutes to 1 hour. To check whether the carrots are cooked, pierce one through the salt pastry with the tip of a knife to see if it is tender.

6 Meanwhile, cook the herby lentils. In a dry frying pan, toast the coriander and cumin seeds for 1–2 minutes until they release their flavour, then grind to a powder in a pestle and mortar. Soften the onion, carrot and celery with the olive oil in a saucepan. Add the toasted and ground spices to the pan and cook for a further 1–2 minutes.

7 Add the lentils and cook for another 2 minutes, pour in the stock to cover, and add half the parsley. Bring to the boil, then reduce the heat and simmer for 25-30 minutes with a lid on until the lentils are tender.

4 tbsp finely chopped
   coriander
4 tbsp finely chopped mint
Grated zest of ½ lemon
Juice of 1 lemon

8 When the lentils are cooked, add the remaining chopped herbs, lemon zest and juice. Season with salt and pepper, and dress with a little olive oil. Cover and set aside, keeping warm until ready to serve.

9 Next, mix the yoghurt with the lemon juice, season with salt and pepper and set aside until ready to serve.

10 When the carrots are cooked, remove from the oven and leave to rest for 10 minutes in the pastry, then remove and discard the pastry crust.

11 Drizzle the carrots with olive oil and season with pepper. Spoon the lentils into four bowls, place two carrots on top of each, spoon over a good dollop of yoghurt and top with the coriander.

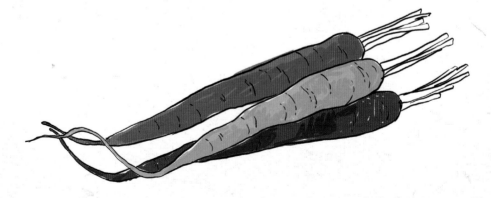

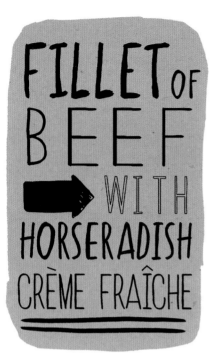

FILLET OF BEEF → WITH HORSERADISH CRÈME FRAÎCHE

This is a great alternative to the traditional way of cooking roast beef on a Sunday. The horseradish crème fraîche is the perfect partner for juicy medium-rare beef.

SERVES 4

FOR THE BEEF
600g beef fillet
Olive oil
Salt and pepper

FOR THE SALT-CRUST
PASTRY
300g coarse sea salt
500g plain flour, plus extra for
    dusting
1 tbsp rosemary, finely
    chopped
300ml warm water

FOR THE HORSERADISH
CRÈME FRAÎCHE
200g crème fraîche
3tbsp finely grated
    horseradish
Squeeze of lemon juice

1. Preheat the oven to 220°C/200°C fan/gas mark 7.

2. Heat a good drizzle of olive oil in a large frying pan over a medium–high heat and sear the beef on all sides until it is a nice brown colour. Remove from the pan to rest for 10 minutes.

3. In a bowl, mix the salt, flour and rosemary and gradually mix in the warm water. Work into a rough dough, then turn out onto a floured work surface and knead for 5 minutes until everything is mixed well and you have a smooth dough. Cover with cling film and chill in the fridge for 30 minutes to firm up.

4. Once rested, roll out the pastry to a 35cm x 25cm rectangle that's 0.5cm thick and place onto a lightly oiled baking tray.

5. Season the beef with pepper and place it in the middle of the dough. Fold up the dough so the beef is completely encased and there are no gaps. Trim off the excess dough and discard.

6. Make a small slit in the top of the pastry parcel to allow the steam to escape and bake in the oven for 20 minutes. When cooked, remove from the oven and allow to rest in the pastry for 20 minutes.

7. Meanwhile, mix the crème fraîche with the finely grated horseradish, add a squeeze of lemon juice and season with salt and pepper.

8. When the beef is rested, remove from the pastry crust and discard the crust. Serve with the horseradish crème fraîche.

WARM CELERIAC, CHICORY & PEAR SALAD

SERVES 4 AS A SIDE

FOR THE SALAD

1 large celeriac
50g whole hazelnuts
25g knob of butter
2 pears, peeled and each
    cut into 6 wedges
1 bulb of red chicory, roughly
    shredded
1 tbsp finely chopped mint
1 tbsp finely chopped
    parsley
Grated zest of ½ orange
Salt and pepper

FOR THE SALT-CRUST PASTRY

300g coarse sea salt
500g plain flour, plus extra for
    dusting
300ml warm water

FOR THE DRESSING

2 tbsp olive oil
2 tbsp hazelnut oil
2 tbsp sherry vinegar

Celeriac is an odd-looking vegetable with a mild nutty flavour that is part of the celery family. It's something I only started eating recently, over the last year or so, but now I'm completely addicted. You can serve this as a main meal by itself, or it's also perfect as a side for roast pork – the flavours complement each other very well.

1. Preheat the oven to 200°C/180°C fan/gas mark 6.

2. In a large bowl, mix the salt and flour, and gradually mix in the warm water. Work into a rough dough, then turn out onto a floured work surface and knead for 5 minutes until everything is mixed well and you have a smooth dough.

3. Roll out the dough to a 35cm circle, place the celeriac in the middle and fold up the pastry so the celeriac is completely encased and there are no gaps.

4. Place onto a lightly oiled baking sheet and bake for 1 hour to 1 hour 20 minutes until cooked. To test whether they are ready, insert a skewer through the pastry and into the heart of the celeriac – if it goes in without too much resistance and feels tender, it is ready.

5. When cooked, remove from the oven and leave the celeriac to rest in its pastry case for 5 minutes. Then remove the pastry crust and discard it. Peel the celeriac, cut into 12 wedges and set aside to keep warm (it shouldn't be served too hot).

6. Now prepare the rest of the salad. Toast the hazelnuts in a small dry frying pan on a gentle heat for 1–2 minutes until they release their flavour. Lightly crush them in a pestle and mortar. Heat a large frying pan with a knob of butter, then gently warm the pears. You want to warm them not cook them.

7. When warmed through, remove from the heat and using a slotted spoon drain them and place in a large serving bowl. Add the celeriac, chicory, toasted hazelnuts, mint, parsley and orange zest and mix.

8. In a small bowl, whisk the dressing ingredients, pour over the salad and toss so everything is coated. Season with a little salt and pepper. Serve warm.

SALT-BAKED PORK TENDERLOIN

SERVES 2

400g pork tenderloin,
  trimmed of any fat or
  sinew
Olive oil
Pepper
Roast or boiled potatoes, to
  serve
Autumn Spiced Apple Sauce
  (see page 210), to serve

FOR THE SALT-CRUST PASTRY

125g coarse sea salt
250g plain flour, plus extra for
  dusting
1 egg white, whisked
1 tbsp fennel seeds
100ml warm water

Pork is one of those meats that dries out quite easily, so baking it in a salt-crust pastry is a clever method of making sure it stays really juicy and moist. The pastry itself doesn't get eaten (unless you want a heart attack!); it's just for cooking and gets removed and thrown away before serving. If you like a pink ribbon in your pork, knock 5 minutes off the cooking time. This is great served with my Autumn Spiced Apple Sauce (see page 210).

1. Preheat the oven to 190°C/170°C fan/gas mark 5.

2. First, make the salt-crust pastry. Toast the fennel seeds in a small dry frying pan on a gentle heat for 1–2 minutes until they release their flavour. Tip into a pestle and mortar and grind the seeds to a powder.

3. In a bowl, mix the salt, flour, egg white and fennel seeds and gradually mix in the warm water.

4. Work into a rough dough, then turn the dough out onto a floured work surface and knead for 5 minutes until everything is mixed well and you have a smooth dough. Cover with cling film and chill in the fridge for 30 minutes to firm up.

5. Heat a large frying pan with 1 tablespoon of olive oil over a medium–high heat and sear the pork on all sides for 1–2 minutes. Remove onto kitchen paper to drain all the excess oil.

6. Once rested, roll out the pastry to a 30cm x 15cm rectangle that's 0.5cm thick and place onto a lightly oiled baking tray.

7. Season the pork with pepper and place it in the middle of the dough. Fold up the dough so the pork is completely encased and there are no gaps. Trim off the excess dough and discard.

8. Make a small slit in the top of the pastry parcel to allow the steam to escape and bake in the oven for 30 minutes. When cooked, remove from the oven and allow to rest in the pastry for 10 minutes.

9. When rested, remove the pastry crust and discard. Cut the pork on the diagonal into slices and serve with roast or boiled potatoes and the Autumn Spiced Apple Sauce.

8

PRESE

AT SCHOOL, I WAS REALLY KEEN ON HISTORY. WE STUDIED THE TUDORS,

and how they loved to have feasts and banquets big enough to feed a whole village. When reading about the food they ate I started to learn about preserving. Back then they obviously didn't have fridges and freezers so they found other ways of storing and extending the life of their food. They smoked and cured meats, preserved vegetables in salt or vinegar, and even buried food (but don't fear – I've not included any recipes that require you to dig up your back garden!).

What you will find in this chapter are different types of preserving, from salting and pickling, to potting and making jam, including how to make a zingtastic curd. You have to try my recipe for Dill-cured Salmon, which is my spin on an old Nordic recipe used by fishermen in the Middle Ages. Not only is it a clever way to preserve fish, it also gives it a different flavour and texture, and is a great alternative to buying smoked salmon, saving you an absolute fortune when entertaining or at Christmas time. If you fancy mixing things up, there are many other flavours you can add to the basic salt/sugar cure instead of dill.

A quick note on jellies and marmalades: until recently I wasn't terribly confident making them as I thought they were something that took years to perfect, but I discovered it's all about using the right sugar. I've used caster sugar in my recipes as it's easily available, however if you can get hold of proper jam sugar do use it because it has a higher pectin content, which helps jam to set. The other thing I've learned is that, as with making ice cream, the secret to jam-making comes down to a magic number – 105°C. Your jam must reach this temperature if you want it to set. If I had listened in my school science classes I'd probably be able to explain how this works, but as I'm not a science god we'll just stick with the magic number. One last tip: be super careful when pouring your jammy creations into jars; the mixtures get extremely hot, and sugar burns are not what dreams are made of...

MALT VINEGAR

PICKLED VEGETABLES

I don't know if it's tradition in your house, but in our house Boxing Day just wouldn't be complete without pickled vegetables. You can pickle them for a few hours, or give them up to a week for best results. We usually eat them with chips and cold meats, but you can pop pickled cucumbers in a bun with a homemade burger, or use pickled carrots in salads or to add a nice, sharp edge to pork or chicken. If unopened, the pickles will keep in a sealed jar for 5–6 months.

PICKLED CUCUMBER

MAKES 2 X 500ML JARS

2 whole cucumbers
3 tbsp Maldon sea salt
300ml cider vinegar
150g caster sugar
1 tbsp fennel seeds
1 tbsp black mustard seeds
1 tsp black peppercorns
1 tbsp finely chopped dill

1. Cut the cucumbers in half lengthways, remove the seeds with a teaspoon and discard. Slice the flesh on the diagonal into 2cm-thick slices.

2. Place the cucumber slices in a colander and sprinkle with the salt. Put the colander in the sink or inside a bowl to catch the liquid that is drawn out. Place a bowl or plate on top of the cucumbers to cover and leave for 1 hour.

3. After 1 hour, discard any liquid that's been drawn out, then rinse the cucumber under cold water, drain and pat dry with kitchen paper to get rid of excess water.

4. Place all the ingredients except the cucumber and dill in a large saucepan with 120ml of water, and cook over a gentle heat until the sugar dissolves, then simmer for 5 minutes. Remove from the heat and allow to cool to room temperature in the pan.

5. Divide the cucumber and dill among sterilised jars (see page 198), then pour in the cooled pickling liquid and seal. Leave to pickle for 1 week before using. Once opened you can keep the cucumber for 1 week.

PICKLED ONIONS

MAKES 2 X 500ML JARS

600g baby onions, peeled
   and tops/stalks removed
3 tbsp Maldon sea salt
250ml cider vinegar
125g caster sugar
2 bay leaves, torn up
1 tbsp mustard seeds
1 tsp black peppercorns
1 tsp dried chilli flakes

1. Put the onions in a mixing bowl and add the salt. Mix well, cover and leave overnight. Rinse well and pat dry with kitchen paper, then divide between sterilised jars (see page 198).

2. Place all the other ingredients in a saucepan with 125ml of water and bring to the boil. Once boiling, immediately remove from the heat and allow to cool to room temperature in the pan.

3. Pour the liquid into the jars and seal. Leave to pickle for 1 week before using. Once opened you can keep the onions for up to 1 week.

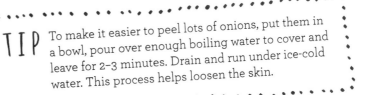

TIP To make it easier to peel lots of onions, put them in a bowl, pour over enough boiling water to cover and leave for 2–3 minutes. Drain and run under ice-cold water. This process helps loosen the skin.

PICKLED CARROTS

MAKES 2 X 500ML JARS

500g carrots, peeled and
    cut into 7cm-long batons,
    1.5cm thick
250ml white wine vinegar
125g caster sugar
1 tbsp caraway seeds
1 tbsp coriander seeds
1 tsp Maldon sea salt
1 shallot, finely sliced
1 red chilli, deseeded and
    finely sliced

1. Bring a large saucepan of water to the boil, add the carrots and cook for 1 minute. Remove, drain and refresh under cold water to stop the cooking process.

2. Place all of the ingredients except the carrots, shallot and chilli in a large saucepan with 125ml of water, and cook over a gentle heat until the sugar dissolves, then simmer for 5 minutes. Remove from the heat and allow to cool to room temperature in the pan.

3. Divide the carrots, shallot and chilli among sterilised jars (see below), then pour in the cooled pickling liquid and seal. Leave to pickle for 1 week before using. Once opened you can keep the pickle for 1 week.

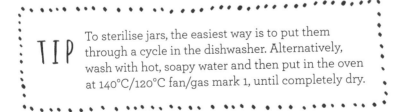

TIP

To sterilise jars, the easiest way is to put them through a cycle in the dishwasher. Alternatively, wash with hot, soapy water and then put in the oven at 140°C/120°C fan/gas mark 1, until completely dry.

MAKES 2 X 500ML JARS

1kg raw beetroot, stalks
    removed, skin left on
125ml red wine vinegar
125ml cider vinegar
125g caster sugar
1 cinnamon stick, broken
    in half
1 tsp black peppercorns
1 tbsp fennel seeds
2 bay leaves, torn up

1. Place the beetroot in a large saucepan and cover with water, bring to the boil then simmer for 45–50 minutes until tender.

2. Remove from the heat, drain and refresh under cold water to stop the cooking process.

3. Peel the beetroot, slice into eighths and divide among sterilised jars (see page 198).

4. Place all the remaining ingredients in a saucepan with 125ml of water and bring to the boil. Once boiling, immediately remove from the heat and allow to cool to room temperature in the pan.

5. Add the liquid to the jars and seal. Leave to pickle for 1 week before using. Once opened you can keep the beetroot for up to 1 week.

SALT BEEF BEIGELS

SERVES 12

FOR THE BEEF
2.5kg beef brisket
2 celery sticks, roughly
    chopped
2 carrots, roughly chopped
1 large onion, peeled and
    halved
2 bay leaves

FOR THE BRINE
500g rock salt
300g light brown
    muscovado sugar
4 thyme sprigs
2 star anise
4 bay leaves
1 tbsp black peppercorns
1 tbsp juniper berries
1 tbsp mustard seeds

TO SERVE
12 bagels, toasted
Butter, for spreading
    (about 100g)
English mustard (optional)
Gherkins (optional)

When I was a kid, my dad would take me and my sister to Brick Lane market every weekend. We'd wander around the stalls buying CDs and odd bits of tat, and on the way home we would stock up on beigels (not 'bagels' as the Americans spell them!) from the famous Brick Lane beigel shop. Here I have created my own spin on their delicious salt beef beigel. When you buy salt beef, it's usually pink because it contains a preservative called saltpetre. As this chemical is also used in gunpowder, I didn't fancy putting it in my version – the salt beef is just as nice without it, but browner in colour.

1. Place all the ingredients for the brine into a large pot with 2.5 litres of water and bring to the boil. Simmer for 5 minutes, then remove from the heat and let it cool to room temperature.

2. Once at room temperature, put the brisket into a large plastic food container and pour in the brine mixture. Weigh down the beef with a plate and put the lid on. Leave for 10 days, turning the beef over once a day and replacing the weight. You can store it in a cold, dry place or in the fridge.

3. After 10 days, when you are ready to cook the beef, remove it from the brine, discard the liquid and rinse the beef thoroughly under a cold tap. Then leave it in fresh water for 15 minutes.

4. Remove the beef from the water and place it in a large cooking pot along with the celery, carrots, onion and bay leaves, and enough fresh water to completely cover it all, then bring to the boil. Once at boiling point, reduce the heat and allow it to simmer uncovered for 3½–4 hours until tender. Every 30 minutes, turn the beef while it's cooking in the pot. You may need to top up the water throughout the cooking time.

5. When the beef is tender, turn off the heat and leave it to cool in the cooking liquor so it can absorb all the flavours. This will take 2–3 hours. You can reserve some of the cooking liquor to reheat the beef in if you wish, or discard it.

6. You can serve the beef cold or reheated, with toasted and buttered bagels, English mustard and gherkins. Store in the fridge for 3–5 days.

POTTED DUCK

MAKES 2 X 250ML JARS

1 tbsp green peppercorns
2 tbsp Maldon sea salt
2 bay leaves, torn up
Leaves from 4 thyme sprigs
½ tsp mace
4 duck legs (approx. 200g
    each)
750ml duck fat, melted
2 tbsp finely chopped
    parsley
4 tbsp cognac

Potting is a great way of preserving many kinds of meat, including game such as venison and rabbit, and shellfish like shrimp and crab. Once the jars are sealed, they make nice presents to give to friends. The soft, shredded flakes of meat are lovely served on toasted sourdough bread with lots of butter.

1. Preheat the oven to 150°C/130°C fan/gas mark 2.

2. Use a pestle and mortar to grind together the green peppercorns, salt, bay leaves, thyme leaves and mace, until well combined.

3. Lay the duck legs in a baking dish and rub the mixture all over them, so the legs are well coated. Pour in the melted duck fat, cover the dish with foil and cook in the oven for 2½ hours until the duck legs are soft and tender.

4. When cooked, remove from the oven and, using tongs, remove the duck legs from the fat (setting it aside for later use) and allow them to cool on a plate for 10 minutes.

5. Once cooled, pick the duck meat off the legs into a mixing bowl, then shred it with a fork and mix in the parsley. Place the meat into jars so that it's tightly packed. Pass the cooking fat through a fine sieve into a bowl, then add the cognac and whisk well to combine. Pour enough fat into each jar so that there are no air bubbles or gaps, then put on the lids and keep sealed until ready to use. This will keep for up to 1 month unopened.

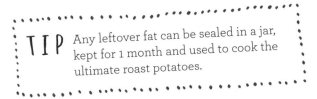

TIP Any leftover fat can be sealed in a jar, kept for 1 month and used to cook the ultimate roast potatoes.

SWEET CHILLI JELLY

MAKES 6 X 190ML JARS

1kg Braeburn or Cox
   apples, peeled, cored and
   cut into rough chunks
25g ginger, peeled and
   roughly sliced
8–10 red chillies (100g
   after deseeding), roughly
   chopped
100ml cider vinegar
750g caster sugar
Grated zest and juice of
   1 lime

EQUIPMENT
Jelly bag or conical sieve
   and muslin

This sweet and tangy jelly is great as a dip for prawns or Asian-style steamed dumplings (see page 46). Try adding finely sliced lemongrass and lime leaves to the mixture, if you fancy giving it more of a Thai flavour.

1. Place the apples and ginger into a large saucepan and add enough water to cover (about 1.2 litres). Bring to the boil and simmer for 30–40 minutes until the apples have become soft and pulpy.

2. Prepare the jelly bag, or line a conical sieve with a clean piece of muslin and put it into another large saucepan or pot. Pour or ladle in the apple mixture. If using the muslin, tie the top in a knot to secure. Leave overnight to allow the liquid to filter through. Do not be tempted to squeeze the apples through the muslin or jelly bag as this will give a cloudy finish to the jelly.

3. Pulse the red chillies in a food processor until finely chopped, then set aside until needed.

4. After the apples have sat overnight, discard the muslin with the apple remains and add the chillies, vinegar, sugar, lime zest and juice to the saucepan of strained apple juice.

5. Place over a gentle heat until the sugar dissolves, then bring to a rapid boil and boil for 15–20 minutes until it reaches 105°C. It's essential to measure the temperature with a cooking thermometer, as this is the precise setting point of the jelly/jam. You need to skim off the scum from the surface regularly with a large spoon and discard. Remove from the heat once it has reached 105°C and leave to cool for a few minutes.

6. Using a funnel, pour the jelly into sterilised jars (see page 198) and leave for a few hours to cool and set. Once set, seal the jars with their lids. The jelly will keep for 1 year unopened.

DILL-CURED SALMON

I created this recipe to share with my family at Christmas. The curing mix looks really festive, with green dill and pink peppercorns lying in a bed of salt that resembles snow. This salmon is ideal for entertaining large numbers of people because it is prepared days in advance, making life a lot easier when your guests arrive. Leftovers keep for up to a week, so you can come back for second helpings on Boxing Day and beyond...

SERVES 6–8

1 tbsp pink peppercorns
300g rock salt
250g caster sugar
35g dill, roughly chopped
Grated zest of 2 lemons
1 side of salmon fillet
    (approx. 1kg), skin on
    and pin-boned

TO SERVE

1 tbsp finely chopped dill
250ml crème fraîche
1 x small jar of cornichons
    (about 340g)
2 lemons, cut into wedges
Rye bread, finely sliced

1. Toast the pink peppercorns in a dry frying pan over a low heat for about 2 minutes until you can begin to smell them. Once toasted, crush them lightly using a pestle and mortar.

2. In a large bowl, mix the crushed peppercorns with the rock salt, sugar, dill and lemon zest until everything is well combined. On a clean work surface, lay out two 50cm lengths of cling film, slightly overlapping by 2–3cm along their long sides, so they make one large sheet. Let the cling film hang over the edge of the work surface so it is easy to roll up.

3. Place the salmon fillet onto the cling film, skin-side down, and pat it dry using kitchen paper. Spread the peppercorn mixture evenly over the fillet.

4. Carefully wrap up the fillet, keeping its shape. Once enclosed, re-wrap in three more layers of cling film.

5. Place the salmon into a roasting tin, then place another roasting tin or baking tray on top of the fish and weigh it down with tins or jars. Chill in the fridge for 3 days.

6. When the salmon has cured for 3 days, remove it from the fridge and unwrap, discarding the cling film and the curing mixture. Rinse under a cold tap to remove the rest of the curing mixture and pat it dry using kitchen paper.

7. To serve, lay the whole fish on a serving board and scatter with chopped dill. Serve the crème fraîche, cornichons, lemons and rye bread alongside for people to assemble as they like.

8. You can store the remaining salmon in the fridge for up to 1 week.

AUTUMN SPICED APPLE SAUCE

MAKES 2 X 250ML JARS

50g unsalted butter
1kg Bramley or cooking
    apples, peeled, cored and
    chopped into 3cm
    chunks
50g golden caster sugar
Juice of 1 lemon
½ tsp cinnamon
¼ nutmeg, freshly grated
6 cloves
½ tsp salt
½ tsp ground black pepper

Roast pork wouldn't be the same without apple sauce, so this is the perfect match for my Salt-baked Pork Tenderloin on page 191 or any other delicious pork roast. The addition of autumn spices adds a great depth of flavour, much nicer than any old jar you can buy in the supermarket.

1 Melt the butter in a saucepan on a gentle heat then add all the remaining ingredients and 100ml of water, place a lid on the saucepan and simmer for about 20 minutes until the apples collapse. You need to stir occasionally to stop it catching on the bottom of the saucepan.

2 Once the apples have collapsed, take the pan off the heat and remove the cloves. Taste to see if more sugar is needed. You may need to add some more if the apples are very tart.

3 Blitz with a hand blender until smooth, then spoon into sterilised jars (see page 198) and seal. This will keep for up to 1 year unopened, or 1–2 weeks in the fridge once opened.

SPICED PLUM CHUTNEY

MAKES 2 X 500ML JARS

1 tbsp olive oil

3 banana or Echalion shallots, finely sliced

1kg plums, stoned and cut into quarters

1 red apple (e.g. Pink Lady or Braeburn), cored and grated

100g currants

2cm piece of ginger, peeled and grated

2 star anise

1 cinnamon stick

1 tsp salt

Good grind of black pepper

250g golden caster sugar

250ml white wine vinegar

100ml port

Squeeze of lemon juice

This chutney is perfect to serve alongside cheese or even duck. You can also make it with damsons instead of plums, which have a sharper flavour and are in season a bit later in the year.

1 Heat the olive oil in a large saucepan over a low heat and gently cook the shallots for 3–4 minutes until tender.

2 Add the plums and cook for a further 1–2 minutes until they are starting to break down. Add the apple, currants, ginger, star anise, cinnamon stick, salt and pepper, and cook for a further 5 minutes on a gentle heat.

3 Add the sugar, vinegar and port and cook for 30 minutes over a gentle heat, stirring every so often so the chutney doesn't catch on the bottom of the pan. If it does start to catch, add a tablespoon or two of water.

4 When thickened, remove the cinnamon stick and star anise and add a squeeze of lemon juice.

5 Remove from the heat and pour into sterilised jars (see page 198). Allow to cool to room temperature and seal. This will keep for up to 1 year unopened, or 1–2 weeks in the fridge once opened.

HOMEMADE PICCALILLI WITH HAM toasties

MAKES 4 X 340ML JARS

FOR THE PICKLING LIQUID

1 tsp celery salt
1 tsp black peppercorns
1 tsp coriander seeds
1 tsp fennel seeds
1 tbsp black mustard seeds
1 cinnamon stick
1 bay leaf
500ml malt vinegar

FOR THE PICCALILLI VEG

1 small cauliflower (approx. 420g), cut into small florets
200g green beans, cut into 1cm pieces
2 shallots, finely sliced
1 large onion, finely diced
1 red pepper, deseeded and cut into 1cm chunks
1 carrot, peeled and cut into 1cm dice
1 chilli, deseeded and finely sliced

FOR THE PICCALILLI SAUCE

250g caster sugar
2 tbsp turmeric
1 tbsp mustard powder
3 tbsp cornflour
1 tsp salt
150ml white wine vinegar

TO SERVE

8 slices of crusty bread, toasted
Butter, for spreading
8 slices of good-quality ham

Piccalilli reminds me of my Aunty Linda. Every weekend when I was young, we would visit my nan and grandad's house and at teatime Aunty Linda would always have a ham sarnie or toastie with piccalilli. Back then I was fascinated by its unique bright-yellow colour, which I eventually discovered is down to mustard powder and turmeric. My piccalilli is sweet and tangy, but not spicy, and just like my Aunty Linda I like it best dolloped on a good old ham toastie!

1. Toast the celery salt and all the spices for the pickling liquid in a dry frying pan over a low heat for 2 minutes. Tip them into a large saucepan along with the malt vinegar and 200ml of water. Bring to the boil, then simmer for 4 minutes. Remove from the heat and allow to cool to room temperature.

2. Put all the prepared vegetables into the liquid and leave them for 24 hours.

3. Once the vegetables have pickled, drain them in a colander and rinse thoroughly under cold water.

4. Discard the cinnamon stick and bay leaf. Bring a saucepan of water to the boil, add the vegetables and cook for 2–3 minutes until firm but tender. Drain the vegetables in a colander and refresh them under cold water to stop the cooking process.

5. Now prepare the piccalilli sauce. Mix the sugar, turmeric, mustard powder, cornflour and salt in a bowl, then add the white wine vinegar and 125ml of water and mix well. In a saucepan, bring this to a boil, then simmer for 15 minutes. You need to stir it every few minutes to make sure it doesn't catch on the bottom of the saucepan.

6. When the sauce has thickened, add the drained vegetables and cook for 5 minutes on a gentle heat.

7. Remove the sauce from the heat and allow to cool, then spoon into sterilised jars (see page 198). The piccalilli will keep in the fridge for 1–2 months.

8. To serve, toast the bread and butter it. Add the ham and finish with a good dollop of piccalilli.

BLOOD ORANGE MARMALADE

MAKES 6 X 190ML JARS

500g blood oranges
   (about 3)
Juice of 1 lemon
1kg caster sugar

Me and oranges are the best of friends. Throughout the *MasterChef* competition I used a lot of oranges, and even made John Torode love them (he hated them before). Here I've given the usual orange marmalade a twist by using beautiful blood oranges. They have a limited season though, available in late winter, so when they aren't around you can use normal oranges instead.

1. Wash the oranges thoroughly and rub them dry.

2. Slice off the tops and bottoms then cut them in half around the middle. Cut into very thin slices and remove any pips.

3. Place into a large cooking pot or saucepan, cover with water and simmer for 1 hour.

4. After 1 hour, bring the oranges up to the boil, add the lemon juice and sugar, and boil for 5 minutes, then leave to simmer for a further 20–25 minutes until the mixture reaches 105°C. It's essential to use a thermometer as the marmalade must reach 105°C in order to set.

5. Remove from the heat and allow to cool for 10 minutes, then spoon into sterilised jars (see page 198). Be very careful, as it will still be extremely hot. This will keep for up to 1 year unopened, or 1–2 weeks in the fridge once opened.

ZINGtAStic LEMON & LIME CURD

Here I've given classic lemon curd a twist by adding limes, which gives it a super zing! It goes really well with my Spelt Scones (see page 111) – perfect for any afternoon tea.

1 Place a large heatproof bowl over a saucepan of simmering water and put the zest and juice of the lemons and limes, the caster sugar and butter in the bowl. Heat until everything has melted and/or dissolved.

2 Whisk the eggs and egg yolk in a separate bowl and pour into the melted mixture, whisking as you go.

3 Keep the water under the bowl simmering on a gentle heat and continue to cook for 15 minutes, stirring every so often until the mixture becomes thick and coats the back of a spoon.

4 Remove from the heat and leave to cool. Divide into sterilised jars (see page 198), seal and store in the fridge for up to 1 week.

MAKES 2 X 250ML JARS

Grated zest and juice of
    2 lemons
Grated zest and juice of
    2 limes
200g caster sugar
100g unsalted butter,
    cubed
3 eggs, plus 1 extra egg
    yolk

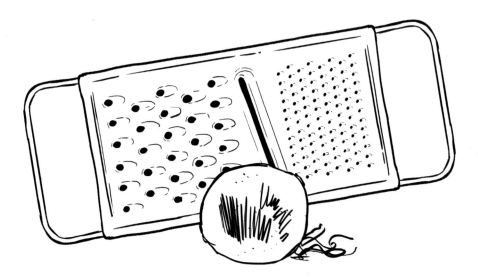

9 FRE

EZING & CHURNING

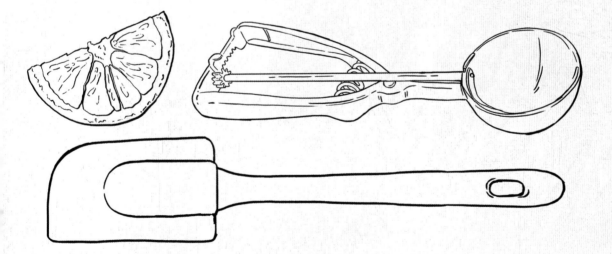

BEFORE I ENTERED *MASTERCHEF* I HAD MANY FAILED ATTEMPTS

at making homemade ice cream. When I got my ice-cream machine I didn't read the user guide (I never normally bother reading the manual for anything and I'm sure I'm not on my own there!), but after a lot of disasters I eventually realised the instructions were there for a reason.

One of my first tries was for my dad's birthday. I'd promised him rum and raisin ice cream, but what he ended up with was a creamy, slushy, rum-spiked, raisin-y mess. Convinced the machine was at fault, or the alcohol content had stopped it from freezing, I went on to attempt a chocolate ice cream, which ended up more like chocolate milkshake. So I temporarily gave up my dreams of making the perfect Mr Whippy, until the MasterChef finals, when I learned a new tip and was brave enough to attempt a milk-flavoured ice cream. It 'seduced' everyone who tried it (their words, not mine), and since that first successful attempt, I've not looked back.

The tip I learned is that 80 is the magic number. You're probably thinking, 'what on Earth are you talking about, Nat?'. Well, when making custard-based ice creams you need to heat the mixture to 80°C, but once it hits that temperature you should remove it from the heat immediately. Another tip when using a custard base is to stir constantly, otherwise you'll end up with scrambled eggs, and I'm sure no one wants scrambled eggs for dessert ... not unless you're Heston. These days my ice-cream machine works like a dream. They say you learn from your mistakes – I certainly have.

As well as ice creams, there are several other frozen treats in this chapter, including a Vodka and Lime Sorbet. Something to remember when making alcohol-based sorbets is not to be too heavy-handed with the booze – if there's too much alcohol the mixture won't set, so try not to get carried away! I've also given you a recipe for frozen yoghurt, which is a healthier treat for a hot summer's day, and some fun smoothie lollies – a brilliant trick to get kids eating one of their 5-a-day without them even knowing it! Use whatever shaped lolly moulds you like – it's all part of the fun.

FLAVOURED ICE CUBES

These ice cubes are perfect for cocktails. Just pop the berry ones into a glass of bubbles and, hey presto, you have an instant berry Bellini! The lemon and lime cubes are great in a gin and tonic, or simply for jazzing up a glass of water.

LEMON & LIME ICE CUBES

Grated zest and juice of
   ½ lemon
Grated zest and juice of
   ½ lime

Pour the ingredients into a small jug with 200ml of water. Mix well and pour the liquid into ice-cube trays. Freeze until set – for a minimum of 4 hours, or preferably overnight.

STRAWBERRY ICE CUBES

200g strawberries, hulled
   and quartered
2 tbsp icing sugar
Squeeze of lemon juice

Blitz all the ingredients in a food processor until you have a smooth purée. Pass through a sieve into a bowl. Pour the liquid into ice-cube trays and freeze until set – for a minimum of 4 hours, or preferably overnight.

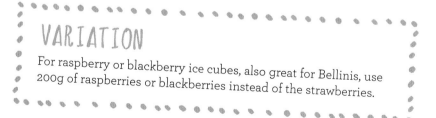

VARIATION

For raspberry or blackberry ice cubes, also great for Bellinis, use 200g of raspberries or blackberries instead of the strawberries.

VANILLA *ICE* CREAM

SERVES 4–6

500ml double cream
250ml whole milk
2 vanilla pods
4 egg yolks
150g caster sugar

This is my basic recipe for rich and creamy vanilla ice cream. Once you've mastered it, you can use it as a starting point to play about with different flavours and invent your own ice cream. Try adding fruit purées, or infusing the cream with various spices, herbs or even teas, instead of the vanilla. Have fun experimenting!

1 In advance, check the instructions for your ice-cream maker in case you need to freeze the bowl overnight before using.

2 Pour the double cream and milk into a large saucepan. Split the vanilla pods lengthways and scrape the seeds into the pan, then add the pods as well. Place on a medium heat until the mixture reaches 80°C (use a cooking thermometer if you have one) or is just before boiling point. Remove from the heat and leave to infuse for 45 minutes.

3 When infused, strain the mixture through a fine sieve into a bowl, discarding the pods, and return to the saucepan.

4 In a mixing bowl, whisk together the egg yolks and sugar until light and fluffy.

5 Heat the milk mixture again until it reaches 80°C or is just before boiling point, then slowly pour it into the bowl of eggs and sugar, whisking as you go. You must keep whisking or you may end up with scrambled eggs. Return the mixture to the saucepan, place on a low heat and stir continuously until it comes back up to 80°C, or just before boiling point, and coats the back of a wooden spoon. Immediately strain through a fine sieve into a bowl and leave to cool to room temperature.

6 Turn on your ice-cream maker 5 minutes before you want to use it, so that when you add the mixture it doesn't stick to the bowl.

7 After 5 minutes, add the mixture and leave it to churn for 35–40 minutes until it reaches a typical ice-cream consistency. Depending on your machine, it may need longer, so refer to the instruction manual and check the mixture often so that it doesn't overchurn – you'll see the machine paddle begin to struggle as the mixture gets too thick. You can serve the ice cream straightaway, or freeze it in a plastic container until required. If freezing, remove it from the freezer 5 minutes before you wish to serve, to allow it to soften slightly.

Chestnut ICE CREAM

SERVES 4–6

200ml whole milk
400ml double cream
300g chestnut jam
    (confiture de châtaignes)
    or 200g chestnut purée
4 egg yolks
75g caster sugar

Back when I was young, in the winter my mum would take me shopping in London's West End. On Tottenham Court Road there was always a man selling roasted chestnuts from a street cart and the smell as you walked past his cart was just amazing. The memory inspired me to create this chestnut ice cream. It's best made with confiture de châtaignes (a chestnut jam) but if you can't get hold of that, chestnut purée also works.

1 In advance, check the instructions for your ice-cream maker in case you need to freeze the bowl overnight before using.

2 In a saucepan, heat the milk, cream and chestnut jam or purée (whichever you are using) over a medium heat until just before boiling point, whisking regularly so the chestnut jam breaks up and dissolves.

3 Meanwhile, whisk the egg yolks and sugar in a large mixing bowl.

4 When the chestnut milk mixture is at 80°C (use a cooking thermometer if you have one) or almost at boiling point, slowly pour it into the bowl of eggs and sugar, whisking constantly. You must keep whisking or you may end up with scrambled eggs. Then pour it all back into the saucepan and return to a medium heat. Still whisking continuously to avoid curdling, cook until the mixture nearly reaches boiling point again (80°C) and is thick enough to coat the back of a spoon. Immediately strain the mixture through a fine sieve into a bowl or jug and leave to cool to room temperature.

5 Turn on your ice-cream maker 5 minutes before you want to use it, so that when you add the mixture it doesn't stick to the bowl.

6 After 5 minutes, add the mixture to the machine and let it churn for 45–50 minutes until it reaches a typical ice-cream consistency. Depending on your machine, it may need longer, so refer to the instruction manual and check the mixture often so that it doesn't overchurn – you'll see the machine paddle begin to struggle as the mixture gets too thick.

7 You can serve the ice cream straightaway or freeze it in a plastic container until required. If freezing, remove it from the freezer 5 minutes before you wish to serve, to allow it to soften slightly.

BASIL ICE CREAM WITH PINK-PEPPERCORN Strawberries

Basil ice cream may seem like madness, but this recipe is the perfect combo of sweet and savoury, with the basil taking on a mellower flavour that is still distinctive. You have to try it to believe it! When I appeared at the Good Food Show, I found an amazing stall selling salt and pepper infused with all kinds of flavours, including a pepper infused with strawberries. It inspired me to try roasting strawberries with peppercorns. The result is another great mix of sweet and savoury, and the perfect partner to my basil ice cream.

SERVES 4–6

FOR THE ICE CREAM

500ml double cream
250ml whole milk
50g basil, roughly
   chopped, plus extra
   to serve
4 egg yolks
150g caster sugar

FOR THE STRAWBERRIES

600g strawberries, hulled
   and halved
3 tbsp golden caster sugar
1 tsp pink peppercorns,
   ground using a pestle
   and mortar
1 tbsp balsamic vinegar

1 In advance, check the instructions for your ice-cream maker in case you need to freeze the bowl overnight before using.

2 Pour the cream and milk into a large saucepan over a medium heat until the mixture reaches 80°C (use a cooking thermometer if you have one) or is just before boiling point, then remove from the heat and add the basil. Leave to infuse for 1 hour.

3 When infused, strain the mixture through a fine sieve into a bowl, discarding the basil, and return to the saucepan.

4 In a mixing bowl, whisk together the egg yolks and sugar until light and fluffy.

5 Heat the milk mixture again until it reaches 80°C or is just before boiling point, then slowly pour it into the bowl of eggs and sugar, whisking as you go. You must keep whisking or you may end up with scrambled eggs. Return the mixture to the saucepan, place on a gentle heat, and stir continuously as it comes back up to 80°C, or just before boiling point, and coats the back of a wooden spoon. Immediately strain through a fine sieve into a bowl and leave to cool to room temperature.

6 Turn on your ice-cream maker 5 minutes before you want to use it, so that when you add the mixture it doesn't stick to the bowl.

CONTINUES

7 After 5 minutes, add the mixture to the machine and let it churn for 35–40 minutes until it reaches a typical ice cream consistency. Depending on your machine, it may need longer, so refer to the instruction manual and check the mixture often so that it doesn't overchurn – you'll see the machine paddle begin to struggle as the mixture gets too thick.

8 If you wish to serve the ice cream straightaway, make the strawberries while the ice cream is churning. Otherwise, you can freeze the ice cream in a plastic container until required. If freezing, remove it from the freezer 5 minutes before you wish to serve, to allow it to soften slightly.

9 Preheat the oven to 200°C/180°C fan/gas mark 6. Place the strawberries in a baking tray, sprinkle with the sugar and ground peppercorns, and drizzle with the balsamic vinegar. Mix well so the strawberries are completely coated and bake for 20 minutes.

10 Remove the softened strawberries from the oven and serve with the basil ice cream. The strawberry syrup left in the baking tray can be drizzled over the strawberries when serving. Decorate with basil leaves, if you wish.

CARDAMOM, ROSE & PISTACHIO ICE CREAM

This recipe was inspired by my publisher Jenny (the big boss!). When talking through ice cream recipes she was like a little child, getting very excited over Middle-Eastern flavours. Somewhere in history, cardamom, rose and pistachio came together in a perfect three-way marriage. I like to add edible rose petals too; this is totally optional, but they do look fab in the finished article.

SERVES 4–6

400ml double cream
200ml whole milk
8 cardamom pods
6 large egg yolks
150g caster sugar
1 tsp rosewater
50g unsalted shelled
    pistachios, roughly
    chopped, plus extra
    to serve
1 tbsp dried edible rose
    petals (optional), plus
    extra to serve

1. In advance, check the instructions for your ice-cream maker in case you need to freeze the bowl overnight before using.

2. Pour the double cream and milk into a large saucepan. Split the cardamom pods and add to the pan. Heat on a medium temperature until it reaches 80°C (use a cooking thermometer if you have one) or is just before boiling point, then turn off the heat and leave to infuse for 45 minutes.

3. When infused, strain the mixture through a fine sieve into a bowl, discarding the pods and seeds, and return to the pan.

4. In a mixing bowl, whisk together the egg yolks and sugar until light and fluffy.

5. Heat the milk mixture again until it reaches 80°C or is just before boiling point, then slowly pour it into the bowl of eggs and sugar, whisking as you go. You must keep whisking or you may end up with scrambled eggs. Return the mixture to the saucepan, place on a gentle heat and stir continuously while it comes back up to 80°C, or just before boiling point, and coats the back of a wooden spoon. Immediately strain through a fine sieve into a bowl and leave to cool to room temperature.

6. Once the mixture has reached room temperature, stir in the rosewater, pistachios and rose petals, if using.

7. Turn on your ice-cream maker 5 minutes before you want to use it, so that when you add the mixture it doesn't stick to the bowl.

8. After 5 minutes, add the mixture and let it churn until it reaches a typical ice-cream consistency. This will take about 35 minutes but depending on your ice cream machine it may need longer, so refer to the instruction manual and check the mixture often so that it doesn't overchurn – you'll see the machine paddle begin to struggle as the mixture gets too thick.

9. You can serve the ice cream straightaway, or freeze it in a plastic container until required. If freezing, remove it from the freezer 5 minutes before you wish to serve, to allow it to soften slightly. Serve with a scattering of pistachios and a few edible rose petals for decoration.

MILK & COOKIE DOUGH ICE CREAM

SERVES 4

FOR THE ICE CREAM
500ml whole milk
80g caster sugar
100ml double cream
100ml condensed milk
1 tbsp liquid glucose
1 gelatine leaf

FOR THE COOKIE DOUGH
75g unsalted butter,
    softened
50g caster sugar
100g plain flour, plus
    extra for dusting
1 tsp vanilla paste
1–2 tbsp whole milk
30g chocolate chips

Milk and cookies was one of my favourite treats as a kid. Combining both of them in an ice cream brings back fond memories of dipping cookies into my milk and getting milk moustaches with my sister! This isn't a custard-based ice cream, but instead uses gelatine and liquid glucose to set the mixture. If you or your guests are vegetarian, you can of course use vegetarian gelatine. Liquid glucose is now available in many supermarket baking aisles; it helps control how the sugar crystallises to make sure your ice cream ends up nice and smooth and not at all grainy.

1 In advance, check the instructions for your ice-cream maker in case you need to freeze the bowl overnight before using.

2 In a large saucepan on a low heat, gently warm the milk and sugar until the sugar has dissolved. Increase the heat and cook for a further 5 minutes, stirring regularly. Reduce the heat to low again and add the cream, condensed milk and glucose. Stir until smooth, then remove from the heat.

3 Meanwhile, soak the gelatine in cold water for about 10 minutes to soften.

4 Drain the gelatine and squeeze it to remove any excess water, then add to the warm milk mixture and stir until completely melted. Leave to cool to room temperature.

5 Turn on your ice-cream maker 5 minutes before you want to use it, so that when you add the mixture it doesn't stick to the bowl.

6 After 5 minutes, pour the cooled mixture into the ice-cream maker and let it churn for 50–60 minutes until it reaches the typical consistency of ice cream. Depending on your machine, it may need longer, so refer to the instruction manual and check the mixture often so that it doesn't overchurn – you'll see the machine paddle begin to struggle as the mixture gets too thick.

7 Meanwhile, make the cookie dough (or you can make this in advance). In a food processor, whiz together the butter and sugar until pale and fluffy. Add the flour, vanilla paste and 1 tablespoon of the milk and blitz. If the dough seems dry, add the other tablespoon of milk and blitz again.

Remove the bowl from the food processor and add the chocolate chips, mixing them in with a spoon so they are evenly spread. Turn out the dough onto a lightly floured work surface and knead gently with your hands until it becomes firm.

 Lay out some cling film and put the dough on top, wrap it up and roll into a cylinder about 14cm long. You want it tightly rolled. Chill in the fridge for 45 minutes to 1 hour to firm up. Before adding the cookie dough to the ice cream, cut it into 1–2cm pieces.

10 When the ice cream is ready, transfer it to a freezer container and fold in the cookie dough pieces. Either serve straightaway or keep it in the freezer until required. If freezing for later, remove it from the freezer 5–10 minutes before serving, to allow it to soften slightly.

COCONUT ARCTIC ROLL WITH ZINGY MANGO

Arctic roll is up there with my all-time favourite childhood puds. This is a tropical spin on the classic dessert that brought so many of us joy when we were small. The zing from the mango adds a nice freshness. If you want to put your own stamp on this recipe, try making it with a different flavour of jam, such as raspberry or strawberry.

SERVES 10

800ml Vanilla Ice Cream
    (see page 224 or use
    good-quality bought)
3 eggs
100g caster sugar, plus
    extra for assembly
75g plain flour
1 tsp baking powder
25g desiccated coconut,
    plus 2 tbsp extra for
    assembly

**FOR THE ZINGY MANGO
JAM (MAKES 400G, BUT
USE ONLY 250G HERE)**
500g peeled ripe mango
    flesh (approx. 2
    mangoes), chopped
    into 1cm chunks
125g caster sugar
Grated zest and juice of
    ½ lime

EQUIPMENT
33cm x 22cm x 2cm Swiss
    roll tin

1 Start by making the mango jam. Place the mango, sugar, lime zest and lime juice in a saucepan and bring to the boil. Continue to boil until the mixture reaches 105°C on a cooking thermometer. It's important to use a thermometer for accuracy here, as 105°C is the precise setting point of the jam.

2 Remove from the heat and allow to cool for 5 minutes then spoon into a jar. You can set aside until ready to use.

3 Next, prepare the centre of the roll. Take the ice cream out of the freezer and let it soften slightly. Lay out two layers of cling film on top of each other, then spoon the ice cream into the centre and roll up tightly, using the cling film, into a 30cm-long sausage shape. Freeze for about 2 hours, until set.

4 For the sponge, preheat the oven to 180°C/160°C fan/gas mark 4. Line the Swiss roll tin with parchment paper.

5 Beat the eggs and sugar in a mixing bowl until pale and fluffy, then sift in the flour and baking powder and fold in with a spatula or metal spoon. When you have a smooth batter, fold in the desiccated coconut until everything is incorporated.

6 Spoon the cake mixture into the tin and flatten evenly, using a spatula or palette knife. Bake for 10–12 minutes until it is set on top – the sponge should feel firm but spring back to the touch. Remove from the oven and allow to cool in the tin for 5 minutes.

7 Dust a sheet of parchment paper with 2 tablespoons of caster sugar. Remove the cake from the tin and flip it out onto the parchment so the cake sits on the sugar. Peel off the paper that lined the tin, which is now stuck to the top of the cake.

8 When the cake is cool, spoon over the mango jam (approx. 250g) until the cake is covered, and sprinkle with 2 tablespoons of desiccated coconut.

9 Unwrap the ice cream sausage and place it on the sponge, 3cm from one of the long edges. Gently roll up, using the paper underneath to help, so that the sponge encases the ice cream completely. Keep the completed Arctic roll wrapped in the parchment paper and return it to the freezer for 4 hours or overnight.

10 When ready to serve, remove from the freezer 10–15 minutes in advance. Just before serving, peel off the parchment and neatly trim the edges.

BLOOD ORANGE GRANITA

SERVES 4

150ml caster sugar
500ml blood orange juice
(from a carton, or
8–9 fresh oranges)
Squeeze of lime juice

A granita is a frozen dessert originally from Sicily. This one is citrusy and refreshing, and really cleanses your palate. You can use other citrus fruits when blood oranges are not in season (they're only available in late winter), and for the adults you can even add a splash of booze, such as Cointreau or vodka.

1. Bring the sugar and 150ml of water to the boil in a saucepan, so that the sugar dissolves. Once boiling, remove from the heat and allow to cool to room temperature.

2. Whisk in the blood orange juice and lime juice and pour the mixture into a metal tray with a rim. Freeze for a minimum of 4 hours until set, or preferably overnight.

3. When ready to serve, break up the granita with a fork into fluffy ice crystals.

SMOOTHIE LOLLIES

**MAKES 4 LARGE OR
8 SMALL LOLLIES**

1 banana, peeled and
    broken up into 2.5cm
    chunks
100g blueberries
100g raspberries
100g strawberries, hulled
1 tsp honey
5 tbsp natural yoghurt
Squeeze of lemon juice

EQUIPMENT
4 x large lolly moulds
    (80–100ml) or 8 x small
    moulds (60ml)

This is a clever way to get kids eating a couple of their
5-a-day without them even knowing! It's also perfect for
using up fruit that is just on the turn.

 Blitz all the ingredients in a food processor or juicer until
smooth. Taste the mixture for sweetness, as you may need to
add some more honey and blitz again, depending on the fruit.

2 Pass the mixture through a sieve into a measuring jug to
remove the pips/seeds. Fill each lolly mould to the top, then
freeze for 4 hours, or preferably overnight, to set.

3 To serve, remove from the mould when set and eat straightaway.

PIMM'S LOLLIES

**MAKES 4 LARGE OR
8 SMALL LOLLIES**

100ml Pimm's
300ml lemonade
Grated zest of ½ lemon
5 mint leaves, finely
    shredded
2 large strawberries,
    hulled and quartered
8 raspberries

EQUIPMENT
4 x large lolly moulds
    (80–100ml) or 8 x small
    moulds (60ml)

Summer wouldn't be the same without Pimm's. This
lolly for grown-ups is the perfect way to cool down
on an English summer's day.

1 Mix the Pimm's, lemonade and lemon zest in a measuring jug.

2 Divide the mint, strawberries and raspberries evenly between
the lolly moulds and pour in the Pimm's mixture to the top of
each mould. Freeze for 4 hours to set.

3 To serve, remove from the mould when set and eat straightaway.

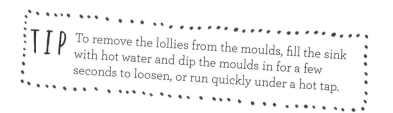

TIP To remove the lollies from the moulds, fill the sink
with hot water and dip the moulds in for a few
seconds to loosen, or run quickly under a hot tap.

VODKA & LIME SORBET

SERVES 4

750g caster sugar
75ml vodka
Grated zest and juice
of 6 limes

Serve this boozy sorbet to your guests and pretend you're Tom Cruise in *Cocktail*! You can replace the lime with lemon or even grapefruit if you fancy mixing it up a bit. Sorry kids, this one is for adults only...

1 In advance, check the instructions for your ice-cream maker in case you need to freeze the bowl overnight before using.

2 Bring the sugar and 750ml of water to the boil in a saucepan, then simmer on a low heat for 5 minutes. Remove from the heat and allow to cool to room temperature.

3 Add the vodka, lime zest and juice and mix well.

4 Turn on your ice-cream maker 5 minutes before you want to use it, so that when you add the mixture it doesn't stick to the bowl.

5 After 5 minutes, add the mixture to the machine and let it churn for 35–45 minutes until it reaches sorbet consistency. Depending on your machine, it may need longer, so refer to the instruction manual and check the mixture often, so it doesn't overchurn – you'll see the machine paddle begin to struggle as the mixture gets too thick.

6 You can serve the sorbet straightaway or freeze it in a plastic container until required. If freezing, remove from the freezer 5 minutes before you wish to serve, to allow it to soften slightly.

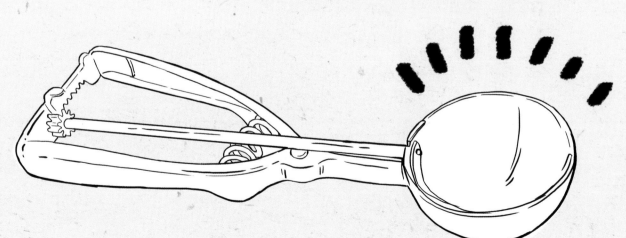

FROZEN GREEK YOGHURT with BAKED FIGS

This is healthier than most ice creams, so you don't have to feel too guilty about tucking in. Frozen yoghurt is so easy to make – it takes less than 5 minutes to prepare, then your ice cream machine does the rest. You can add your favourite flavours to taste, but I like a little bit of honey and lemon juice to tame the sourness.

1. Preheat the oven to 180°C/160°C fan/gas mark 4.

2. In advance, check the instructions for your ice-cream maker in case you need to freeze the bowl overnight before using.

3. Using a wooden spoon, mix together the yoghurt, lemon juice, honey and vanilla paste in a mixing bowl. You may wish to add more honey, lemon or vanilla according to taste, but the yoghurt should be quite sharp to offset the sweetness of the baked figs.

4. Turn on your ice-cream maker 5 minutes before you want to use it, so that when you add the mixture it doesn't stick to the bowl.

5. After 5 minutes, add the yoghurt mixture to the machine and let it churn until it reaches a consistency similar to that of ice cream. This will take about 30 minutes but depending on your machine it may need longer, so refer to the instruction manual and keep checking the mixture so that it doesn't overchurn – you'll see the machine paddle begin to struggle as the mixture gets too thick.

6. If you wish to serve the frozen yoghurt straightaway, make the figs while the mixture is churning. Otherwise, you can freeze the yoghurt in a plastic container until required. If freezing, remove it from the freezer 5 minutes before you wish to serve, to allow it to soften slightly.

7. To prepare the figs, cut off the stems, then slice a cross into each fig so it is still intact but opens up into quarters. (If your figs are very small, you can just halve them.) Place in a baking dish and drizzle with the honey. Bake for 20 minutes or until soft. Remove from the oven and serve along with the frozen yoghurt and crushed pistachios, drizzled with more honey and scattered with mint, if using.

SERVES 4

FOR THE FROZEN YOGHURT
700g natural Greek yoghurt
Juice of ½ lemon
6 tbsp honey
2 tbsp vanilla paste

FOR THE BAKED FIGS
4 large figs
1 tbsp honey

TO SERVE
25g unsalted shelled pistachios, roughly chopped
Honey, for drizzling
5 mint leaves, finely chopped (optional)

RICOTTA ICE CREAM WITH ROASTED CHERRIES

SERVES 4

FOR THE ICE CREAM
250g ricotta
500ml double cream
2 tbsp honey
1 tsp vanilla paste

FOR THE CHERRIES
225g cherries, stalks
   removed and pitted
2 tbsp golden caster sugar

TO SERVE
50g whole almonds
   (skin on)
Honey, for drizzling
Leaves from 1 thyme sprig
   (optional)

I love desserts that mix savoury with sweet. Some of my friends prefer a cheeseboard to finish a meal, while others always go for dessert, so I came up with this idea to please everyone at once! All the flavours complement each other very well. Try using baked peaches if you fancy a change from cherries.

1 In advance, check the instructions for your ice-cream maker in case you need to freeze the bowl overnight before using.

2 In a mixing bowl, whisk all the ice cream ingredients together so that everything is well combined and the mixture is free of any lumps.

3 Turn on your ice-cream maker 5 minutes before you want to use it, so that when you add the mixture it doesn't stick to the bowl.

4 After 5 minutes, add the mixture to the machine and let it churn for 30–35 minutes until it reaches a typical ice-cream consistency. Depending on your machine, it may need longer, so refer to the instruction manual and check the mixture often so that it doesn't overchurn – you'll see the machine paddle begin to struggle as the mixture gets too thick. You can serve the ice cream straightaway, or freeze in a plastic container until required. If freezing, remove from the freezer 5 minutes before you wish to serve, to allow it to soften slightly.

5 For the cherries, preheat the oven to 180°C/160°C fan/gas mark 4. Place the cherries in a roasting dish and sprinkle with the sugar. Bake for 15–20 minutes until softened but still firm.

6 Meanwhile, put the almonds in a dry frying pan on a low heat and toast for 2–3 minutes until they release their oils/aroma, then crush lightly using a pestle and mortar. You don't want to end up with too-small pieces. Set aside until ready to serve.

7 Once the cherries are ready, remove from the oven and leave to cool slightly until warm rather than hot.

8 When ready to serve, scoop the ice cream into serving bowls, divide the warm cherries evenly and spoon over any cooking juices. Add the crushed almonds, drizzle with honey and scatter with the thyme leaves, if using.

ACKNOWLEDGEMENTS

A BIG THANK YOU to....

My Nan Bella, who kick-started my passion for cooking. Some of my earliest memories are of Sunday baking and making butterfly fairy cakes in her kitchen. She taught me that a good cook can make anything taste good. I wish she were here to see the finished book.

My Grandad Chris, who has been and still is my number one guinea pig. Thanks for your patience during my kitchen meltdowns throughout and after the *MasterChef* competition. I don't know anyone who would put up with midnight tastings or three-course dinners before midday.

My Mum and Dad who are the most supportive and loving parents. Without your support and guidance I wouldn't have been able to make a massive career change into the food world. Also for being two of my most critical tasters.

My sister Carly, for being so supportive and pushy. You continue to push me to be the best. And also for being so fussy; if you eat my creations I know I'm on to a winner.

The rest of my family: Linda, Keith, Danny, Ellen, Ryan, Joe, Leo, Alison, Tom, Maddy, Paddy, Carol, Malcolm, Elsie and Stan, for being the best family I could ask for. I love you guys.

Ed, for being the best friend ever, even when having kitchen tantrums. I know being force-fed new recipes at midnight isn't the norm but thanks for putting up with the madness.

My besties: Vicki, Johnny, Elisha, Candy, John, Dom, Anne Marie, Kerri, Laura, Jo and Rich for understanding me disappearing off the face of the earth for the last year and a half. You guys are the best.

Fresh Partners, Debbie and her 'Angels', Olivia, Lydia and Rachel, for keeping me in check and making sure life runs like clockwork. You guys are invaluable.

Karen Ross, for being so supportive after *MasterChef* and for making so many of my dreams come true.

To John and Gregg, for one of the most amazing experiences of my life and for the continued advice after the competition.

The *MasterChef* crew, for everything throughout filming. You guys rock.

Plank PR: Lou, Bev, Sally, Topazz, Steve, for everything in the *MasterChef* madness. You guys are the best PR team ever.

Stephen, the best office boss I ever had. Thanks for being the coolest and allowing me six weeks off work to chase my dream.

Jenny Heller, for being the best publisher you could ask for. You saw the method behind the madness and helped me focus on one thing rather than everything.

The Quercus team: Ione, David N, Nick, Paul, Richard, Imogen, Bethan, Hannah R, Caroline B, Caroline P, for being the A-Team. Without you guys this book would not have happened.

David Eldridge and Holly at Two Associates for their amazing design and patience. You made all the dreams in my head a reality.

Bridget, for all the hours of recipe testing and the endless phonecalls. Without you this book would not have come together.

Cristian, the best happy snapper around. You made every snap look like a Van Gogh... Oh, and for introducing popcorn tennis to my life.

Cynthia, the best prop stylist ever. You got my style and everything you brought was so beautiful.

Justine, for being a fab food stylist. You are deffo queen of the splodge and crumb.

Lauren and Sam, for all your hard work on the shoot.

All the restaurants I have 'staged' at: Le Gavroche, Viajante, Marcus Wareing at The Berkeley, The Hand and Flowers, The Kitchin, Castle Terrace, L'Enclume, St John's, Midsummer House, The Gilbert Scott, The Tapas Revolution and Theo Randall at The Intercontinental. For allowing me to come into your kitchens. I really appreciate your time and everything I learnt whilst staging.

All the Borough Market traders, for being so helpful and opening my eyes to some of the best produce in the world.

Quercus Editions Ltd
55 Baker Street
7th Floor, South Block
London W1U 8EW

First published in 2014

A catalogue record of this book is available from the British Library

ISBN 978 1 84866 620 7

Publishing Director: Jenny Heller
Editor: Ione Walder
Art Director: Nick Clark
Design, illustration and cover: Two Associates
Photography: Cristian Barnett
Food styling: Justine Pattison
Prop styling: Cynthia Inions
Copyediting: Sarah Chatwin
Project management: Imogen Fortes

Printed and bound in Portugal